THE FOOLISHNESS OF PREACHING

THE FOOLISHNESS OF PREACHING

Proclaiming the Gospel against the Wisdom of the World

The George Craig Stewart Lectures for 1996
Seabury-Western Theological Seminary

ROBERT FARRAR CAPON

WILLIAM B. EERDMANS PUBLISHING COMPANY
GRAND RAPIDS, MICHIGAN / CAMBRIDGE, U.K.

© 1998 by Robert Farrar Capon
Published by Wm. B. Eerdmans Publishing Co.
255 Jefferson Ave. S.E., Grand Rapids, Michigan 49503 /
P.O. Box 163, Cambridge CB3 9PU U.K.

Printed in the United States of America

03 02 01 00 99   7 6 5 4 3 2

Library of Congress Cataloging-in-Publication Data

Capon, Robert Farrar.
The foolishness of preaching: proclaiming the Gospel
against the wisdom of the world / Robert Farrar Capon.
         p.   cm.
— (The George Craig Stewart lectures for 1996)
ISBN 0-8028-4305-0 (pbk.: alk. paper)
1. Preaching.   I. Title.
II. Series: George Craig Stewart lectures; 1996
BV4211.2.C265   1998
251 — dc21   97-39592
                                        CIP

1 Corinthians 1:21

Ἐπειδὴ γὰρ ἐν τῇ σοφίᾳ τοῦ θεοῦ οὐκ ἔγνω ὁ κόσμος διὰ τῆς σοφίας τὸν θεόν, εὐδόκησεν ὁ θεὸς διὰ τῆς μωρίας τοῦ κηρύγματος σῶσαι τοὺς πιστεύοντας.

For since, in the wisdom of God, the world did not know God through wisdom, God decided, through the foolishness of our proclamation, to save those who believe.

Contents

A Word in Advance

Though I've spent my entire life and ministry in the Episcopal Church, I'm afraid that's a less-than-glowing credential to offer at the beginning of a book on preaching. My ecclesiastical home has seldom been famous for its homiletical cooking — and even more rarely for the time its cooks devote to preparing their dishes: "short shrift" is the phrase that describes too many of our sermons. An old priest I once knew used to say (apropos the mini-preachments, if any, that were given at the eight o'clock Eucharist in his day), "Sermonettes make christianettes." The situation among us has gotten somewhat better since then (we now have "homilies" at eight); but since it still isn't what it ought to be, this book will be my contribution toward improving it.

However, my words are not just for Episcopalians but for both clergy and lay persons who live in other households as well. I have in mind not only the few star preachers who have a consuming interest in preparing sermons but also the working stiffs (sometimes eleventh-hour workers, and sometimes literally stiff) who must stand in the pulpit every Sunday and try to say something useful in the Name of the Father, the Son, and the Holy Spirit. Moreover, I've aimed this book at ecclesiastical homes that range from "high" to "low." I want to speak to those of you who place heavy emphasis on the liturgy of the church catholic: to Roman Catholics, Episcopalians, and Lutherans. But I also think I may have something helpful to say to those who sit looser to that tradition — Presbyterians, Methodists, Disciples of Christ, Baptists, . . . (you fill in the blank). So in whatever Church you find yourself — and on whichever side of the pulpit desk — I invite you to join me in a chat.

As you see, I'm being careful not to overlook the *laity* of the various churches. You who sit in the pews are just as much involved in preaching as the clergy. In most cases, you hire them to be your pastors. And in all cases, you hear them, evaluate them, and even give them the occasional piece of your mind — indeed, in desperate cases, you wish they would simply get lost. So don't put this book down when you come to the end of my more general remarks about preaching in Part One. The practical advice to preachers in Part Two has been written with you in mind as well. Perhaps it will give you a better idea of what's supposed to be involved in the preparation of sermons. Perhaps it will make your criticisms of them more discerning — even helpful. But my profoundest hope is that perhaps you'll get your sights lined up more accurately on what and what not to look for the next time your church has an empty pulpit to fill. You are by far the largest group responsible for the preachers who have sunk us in our present homiletical quagmire, and you are the most likely group to get us out of it.

(Just one preliminary note for preachers in particular. In my previous books, I've always transliterated my references to the Greek of the New Testament into English characters. Here, though, in the hope of inspiring you to go back to the original documents rather than depend on the stack of often undependable versions on your desk, I've left them in Greek. It won't kill you to *wrestle* a bit. Trust me; it will do you good.)

Shelter Island, New York   Robert Farrar Capon
Summer 1997

PART ONE

THE BEDROCK
OF PREACHING

ONE

Passion Play

Let me begin without ceremony. I'd like you to join me in a little theological dabbling. We're going to be roughing in the scenario for a short film intended to depict what the Gospel claims God has done for us in Christ — a film that will use the figure of a lifeguard as a stand-in for Jesus. Here are a few notes I've jotted down as a first draft.

While the credits are rolling, the camera pans slowly along a crowded ocean beach on a bright Saturday afternoon. Insistent rock music plays over the scene. We see that the surf is up and that the lifeguard is busy ordering people out of the water. When they're all out, he returns to his lifeguard tower and puts up the "No Swimming" sign. We hear the crowd on the sand complain briefly but then good-naturedly settle for sun-bathing and picnicking instead of tempting fate. Suddenly, though, one of them spots a teenage girl waving frantically a hundred yards off shore. The music fades and the action begins.

But stop right there. If we're going to fulfill our purpose, we have to make a decision about where the action is going. One way we could decide would be to ask ourselves what the characters in the film would want to happen. On the assumption that the crowd, the lifeguard, and the girl are a typical twentieth-century mix of Christians, Jews, Agnostics, Atheists, and What Have You, the answer to that one is easy: they'll want the lifeguard/Christ figure to come down from his perch, swim gallantly out to the girl, and tow her back to the safety of the beach. They'll put up with a little tension for cinematic effect (the girl can be unconscious when the lifeguard brings her out of the water; the crowd can begin to wonder if the CPR is going to work). Eventually, though, she'll revive, and the film will end with cheers for the lifeguard and pious expressions of gratitude that the girl isn't dead. But then we'll have to work in a few "six-o'clock-news" shots of reporters thrusting microphones in the faces of bystanders who spout the usual object lessons: "The girl was a fool." "She broke the rules." "People like that are just lucky they don't get what they deserve." "Johnny, I hope that'll teach you not to play chicken with the forces of nature." In short, this version of the remainder of my first draft would give us the Good News as a successful rescue there and then on the beach, followed by a long afternoon of value judgments.

Yet if we do it that way, we're faced with a second question: Is that crowd-pleasing scenario of "salvation" in any way relevant to what the Gospel says God has done for us in Jesus? If we're going to be honest, I'm afraid we both know it isn't. As a matter of fact, I think that if we're going to try seriously to make our film a fair metaphor for the Good News, the script will have to be radically rewritten. Watch while I make the necessary changes (and incidentally, reformat the script as a more typical screenplay).

EXTERIOR — OCEAN BEACH on a sunny afternoon.

As the CREDITS ROLL, we HEAR rock music and we PAN SLOWLY across the large crowd on the beach. We ZOOM IN ON A LIFEGUARD sitting on his tower and talking with some GIRLS, and we HEAR snatches of the conversation.

GIRL #1 You really have to make everybody get out of the water?

LIFEGUARD 'Fraid so. The surf's getting stronger and there's a bad undertow.

GIRL #2 Bummer! This is my only weekend out here.

LIFEGUARD (*hanging up the* NO SWIMMING *sign and getting down from the tower*) Better luck next time. It's just not safe.

> We FOLLOW THE LIFEGUARD down to the water's edge, and we HEAR HIM begin ordering people out of the surf. OVERHEAD — CROSS-CUTTING BETWEEN THE LIFEGUARD and THE SWIMMERS:

LIFEGUARD (*blowing his whistle and shouting by turns*) C'mon! Everybody out! It's getting too dangerous.

SWIMMER #1 Do we have to? Why can't we just stay in the shallow part?

LIFEGUARD (*becoming annoyed*) Because I said you can't. Move it!

SWIMMER #2 (*coming out and talking to his companion*) How to ruin a nice day! I don't think it's all that bad.

LIFEGUARD (*overhearing*) Trust me, it is. Out!

SWIMMER #2 (*coming out of the water*) All right already! I thought this was a free country.

LIFEGUARD Not on my beach!

> WE FOCUS ON THE LIFEGUARD after everybody seems to be out of the water. We FOLLOW HIM as he starts to walk back to his tower, and we PAN ACROSS THE CROWD as they begin to settle down to picnicking and sunbathing. CREDITS END and MUSIC FADES.
>
> We REVERSE ON A TEN-YEAR-OLD BOY who is waving frantically and pointing out to sea.

BOY Hey, look! Look! There's still somebody out there!

We PAN OUT OVER THE SURF to a GIRL struggling in the swells about 100 yards out. We ZOOM IN ON THE GIRL, and we SEE HER alternately going under and coming up flailing her arms.

GIRL Help! Help!

We REVERSE ON THE LIFEGUARD as he jumps down from the TOWER, and we FOLLOW HIM as he runs to the WATER, dives in, and starts to swim out to THE GIRL.

CROSS-CUTTING BETWEEN THE LIFEGUARD and THE CROWD that begins to gather at the water's edge:

CROWD MEMBER #1 How in the world did he miss her?

CROWD MEMBER #2 You think he'll get to her in time?

CROWD MEMBER #3 I certainly hope so. [Editorial note from RFC: To this point, we've made no substantial alterations in the script. From here on out, however, drastic changes will be necessary.]

We REVERSE ON THE LIFEGUARD as he reaches THE GIRL. There is NO DIALOGUE between them. We HOLD FOR A GOOD MANY BEATS on them, and we SEE THE LIFEGUARD go under and not come up. We HOLD ON THE GIRL FOR MANY MORE BEATS, and we SEE her go under as well. We HOLD ON THE SWELLS long enough to establish that they have both drowned; then we REVERSE ON THE CROWD:

CROWD MEMBER #1 What's happening?

CROWD MEMBER #2 I can't see them!

CROWD MEMBER #1 Why aren't they coming up?

CROWD MEMBER #3 You think they've both drowned?

CROWD MEMBER #4 It can't be!

CROWD MEMBER #2 I hate to say it, but I think it's true.

CROWD MEMBERS GENERALLY (*overlapping one another*)

Oh, no!

It's horrible!

I don't believe this! It's weird! Just this morning I had the strongest feeling something bad was going to happen.

How can God just stand by and let people die like that?

How awful!

> While THE CROWD is still talking, we PAN TO THE LIFEGUARD TOWER. We ZOOM IN ON A CLIPBOARD left lying on the SEAT.
>
> CLOSE-UP ON THE CLIPBOARD; a NOTE reads: "IT'S ALL OKAY. TRUST ME, SHE'S SAFE IN MY DEATH."
>
> We REVERSE SLOWLY to a LONG SHOT OF THE OCEAN. We SEE no one, and we HOLD ON THE EMPTINESS.
>
> FADE TO BLACK.

TWO

A Passion for the Passion

Now then: What, you may ask, does that *noir* little exercise have to do with preaching? As far as I'm concerned, practically everything. What pass for sermons among us are far too often trite remakes of the film that would have come out of our *first draft* of the lifeguard scenario, when what sermons ought to be are faithful productions of the off-putting *screenplay* we eventually came up with.

For one thing, our preachers tell us the wrong story entirely, saying not a word about the dark side — no, that's too weak — about the dark *center* of the Gospel. They can't bring themselves to come within a country mile of the horrendous truth that we are saved in our *deaths*, not by our efforts to lead a good life. Instead, they mouth the canned recipes for successful living they think their congregations want to hear. It makes no difference what kind of success they urge on us: "spiritual" or "religious" success is as irrelevant to the Gospel as is success in health, money, or love. Nothing counts but the *cross*. But for an even sadder thing, on the rare occasions when they do get around to proclaiming the outrageousness of salvation by the death of the divine Lifeguard, they can do it for no more than fifteen minutes. In the last five minutes of the sermon they meekly take back with the right hand of plausibility everything they so boldly set forth with the left hand of paradox.

Congregations are equally guilty. Preaching is a two-way street: what is said in a sermon depends every bit as much on the listeners as it does on the preacher. If the folks in the pews are constantly running old, happy-ending films inside their heads, they'll make sure he or she gets the message that they're not going to sit still for anybody who tries to sell them a dead God on the cross. The *incompetence* of it all is just too much for them. True enough, there are exceptions on both sides of the homiletical street: there are congregations who will be open to the craziness of genuine Gospel preaching, and there are preachers who will proclaim the foolishness and weakness of God in Christ even if nobody listens. But they're few and far between. Most of what's expected from sermons, on both sides of the pulpit light, is nothing but a thick, soggy blanket thrown over the only Good News there is: the *Passion* of Jesus.

Hence the text I chose for the epigraph of this book: *"For since, in the wisdom of God, it never worked out that the world knew God by its own wisdom, it pleased God, by the foolishness of the proclamation* [of the cross], *to save those who trust"* (my translation). For my money, the root of preaching for our time remains what it was for Paul: *a passion for the Passion.* Like him, those who stand up to preach in the church must decide to "forget everything except Jesus Christ, and him crucified" (1 Cor. 2:2). However macabre it may seem to hold up death and not life as the instrument of salvation, any other proclamation than that is rootless and withered. However foolish or weak such preaching may sound, it celebrates the only wisdom or power that has anything to do with the desperate case of the human race.

A passion for the Passion, then: A passion of the preacher's heart for Jesus himself — a wild romance with the Person of the incarnate Word who reigns in death at the roots of the being of every creature, bar none. A passion of the preacher's soul for the divine Vulgarity that stands caution on its head and takes all the riffraff of the world home free by making the one ticket everybody has the only ticket anybody needs. And a hilarious passion — a bright fire in the preacher's belly — for the sheer fun of shocking the troops awake with the astonishing news that God has torn up his membership card in the God Union, that he has stopped counting the world's trespasses, and that to be raised up into the new creation, we don't need to be good, holy, smart, accountable, or even faithful: we need only to be *dead*.

Obviously, such passion for the Passion is conspicuous in our pulpits chiefly by its absence. But to understand why, we have to go back to our two versions of the lifeguard scenario. The fundamental conflict between them is that the first draft of the film pleases us because it gives us the *reasonable outcome* we feel we have every right to expect, while the screenplay for the final *film noir* baffles us with an *implausible mystery*. Our problem with them, you see, is not that we prefer the first because it has a happy ending and is a comedy, or that we detest the second because it has a sad ending and is a tragedy. Until we get further into either scenario, any decision about comedy or tragedy is premature.

The first thing to note is that our earlier, Lifeguard-Saves-Girl-From-Death scenario fails to measure up to the standard of even a middling comedy. Despite its gratifying conclusion, the "world" of the first draft of the film — the *historical context* in which it operates — is hardly happier as a result of the girl's "salvation": At the end, the characters go back to being the same old people they were at the beginning. The lifeguard returns to his routine of chatting up girls and exposing himself to radiation; the members of the crowd go home to their humdrum lives and boring opinions; and the girl . . . well, I want to hold off on her for a moment. Because none of that unaltered normalcy is the way proper comedy works. In a good comedy, as in a good fairy tale, there is a promise of *cosmic* change at the end: The total and mystical newness of Cary Grant and Grace Kelly in *To Catch a Thief*, for example, is proclaimed by the fireworks display outside their bedroom window. The Princess and the Miller's Third Son who revived her from a hundred years' sleep "live happily ever after" in the mystery of his late-revealed kingship.

But no such promise is fulfilled for the girl in our first scenario. She is delivered from death by drowning on a sunny Saturday afternoon, yes. But she is not delivered from the rest of a lifetime of failed romances, dead-end marriages, or abusive men; from cancer, migraines, arthritis, or bad hair days; or, to clinch the point, from her own absolutely certain death on a cloudy day a week after her eighty-first birthday. In short, the story is devoid of any *historic* significance. It's not a comedy. It's just the *chronicle* of an odd job well done — of something with no more permanent importance than a successful trip to Wal-Mart for a birthday card, three undershirts, and five pounds of potatoes. It's not even *miraculous,* for crying out loud!

Allow me a short digression. There are a number of such scenarios in the stories told about Jesus' miracles: sight restored to the blind on a few occasions, a clutch of deranged people straightened out by exorcism, three dead bodies raised, two spectacular feedings, and one gratuitous production of 180 gallons of wine for a wedding reception whose celebrants were already three sheets to the wind. But none of those miracles was a *program* for fixing up history: most of the blind of Jesus' time went on being blind; Lazarus rose only to die again another day; lepers are still with us; and the descendants of the bridegroom at the wedding received no guarantee of a full wine-cellar in perpetuity. As *salvation scenarios,* they're a bust.

To the Gospel writers' credit, they're never presented to us as such. John, for example, makes it quite clear that those "miracles" were not Jesus' program; they were simply *signs* of it. (The word "miracle" is a misleading translation of σημεῖον, "sign," which is the word that John in particular uses.) The program itself, when Jesus does get around to revealing it, turns out to be nothing but *himself in his death and resurrection.* For all practical purposes, however, that leaves us with just his death as the *knowable* part of the program. True enough, his resurrection does claim to repair our history *mysteriously.* But since it hasn't ameliorated our disasters *materially,* we're stuck with a paradoxical pig in an off-putting poke indeed — with *trusting* an unprovable assertion wrapped in an unacceptable offer.

That's why (to end the digression) our final screenplay does much better. It gives us EMPTINESS, and it FADES TO BLACK after the lifeguard's death. The sole "resurrection" in it is the mysterious NOTE ON THE CLIPBOARD at the end. That's also why it is a mistake to move too quickly from Jesus' death to his resurrection. The danger is that we will be tempted to see it as a mere plausibility — as a kind of *transaction* that does a patch job on history at certain times and places. But the empty tomb is not a program of temporal rescue executed by a beach hero; it's the NOTE left by the dead divine LIFEGUARD. That's why I think Jesus rounds out his resurrection appearances by getting out of town at the ascension. If he'd hung around to the end of time, people would assume that if they could get in touch with him, he would do a similar patch job on them. However, since the whole thrust of Paul, not to mention the rest of the New Testament, is that the job is *already done* (SHE'S SAFE IN MY DEATH), he ups and leaves lest they think they have to hunt for him in Scranton or Buenos Aires.

Do you see? It's not until you get that deeply into the screenplay version of the lifeguard story — or into the Gospel story itself — that you can begin to talk about comedy or tragedy. If you don't trust the promise of the NOTE, then you're stuck with another of life's meaningless tragedies: history goes on unrepaired — so what else is new? But if you trust it, it's the best comedy there is. The mess of history is fixed once and for all in the mystery of death. Happily Ever After has arrived.

But the most passionately wonderful thing about it is the way it delivers you, as a preacher, from having to spout uplifting hokum from the pulpit. No useless programs of life improvement need ever pass your lips; no empty threats about what will happen to your people if they don't improve will ever insult their intelligence, or yours. You won't have to tell them that love will make their lives soar upward like eagles, if only they'll work harder at it. That's a lie. It's precisely their efforts at love that have given their lives the glide angle of a dump truck; and it's the disasters of those efforts — the crucifixions to which their loves inexorably lead — that are their salvation from the road accidents of their history. You won't have to warn them that they must stop sinning if they want God to like them. That's another lie. In their death, by Jesus' death, their sins are no problem for the God who has taken away the handwriting that was against them and nailed it to his cross (Col. 2:14). Above all, you won't even have to tell them they need to be morally upright to earn God's favor. That's the biggest, bad-news lie of all, because God has gone and accepted every last one of them in his beloved Son and is as pleased as punch with them in Jesus. If you can make up your mind, when you go into the pulpit, to forget everything except Jesus Christ and him crucified, you'll have nothing to give them but *Good News*.

They have struggled all their lives against the fear of being last, lost, least, little, or dead — and not one of them has moved an inch away from any of those conditions. Your vocation, your passion, your whole reward is to convince the frantic winners in your congregation to trust that those very conditions are their *personal sacraments* of Jesus' presence — and that IT'S ALL OKAY: THEY'RE SAFE IN HIS DEATH. The only trick is, you'll first have to trust it yourself, *passionately*.

THREE

Stumbling Blocks

We've arrived (if not without warning, then at least abruptly), at the matter of the *personal faith* of the preacher in Jesus Christ, and him crucified. Let me come at it obliquely.

I think good preachers should be like bad kids. They ought to be naughty enough to tiptoe up on dozing congregations, steal their bottles of religion pills, spirituality pills, and morality pills, and flush them all down the drain. The church, by and large, has drugged itself into thinking that proper human behavior is the key to its relationship with God. What preachers need to do is force it to go cold turkey with nothing but the word of the cross — and then be brave enough to stick around while it goes through the inevitable withdrawal symptoms. But preachers can't be that naughty or brave unless they're free of their own need for the dope of *acceptance.* And they won't be free of their need until they can trust the God who has already accepted them, in advance and dead as doornails, in Jesus. *Ergo,* the absolute indispensability of *trust in Jesus' Passion:* unless the faith of preachers is in that alone — and not in any other person, ecclesiastical institution, theological system, moral prescription, or master recipe for human loveliness — they will be of very little use in the pulpit. *Q.E.D.*

Sadly, there are a lot of preachers plying the trade who are not useful. That's because they're afraid, for one non-Gospel reason or another, to be *fools for Christ's sake.* They spend their entire "careers"

14

struggling to be winners: they never kick the habit long enough to find the foolishness of Jesus in their inevitable losing. But life has a surprise in store for them. As they overdose their way through the pursuit of success, they gradually become the very thing they most feared anyway: they turn into *just plain fools*, for Chrissake!

We've all seen their dismal progress. New preachers, green from seminary and ordination, generally have impudent minds and fresh mouths. They don't usually have luxuriously furnished intellects or great deliveries; but they frequently have enough delight in the foolishness of winning by losing (and so many reminders that they themselves are losers) that they qualify as useful representatives of the Ultimate Loser. Give them a couple of years in a parish church, though — or a sequence of increasingly "important" pulpits — and most of them will become like the rest of us: winners for whom losing is the ultimate terror. Curates, Assistants, Youth Ministers, and most of the other Clergy of Low Estate sooner or later become Rectors, Senior Pastors, Bishops, and Ecclesiastical Bureaucrats. All too commonly (since there's not a lot of room in any profession at the pinnacle of the *cursus honorum*), they end up as priests or ministers in places like Resume Speed, Indiana — or bishops of dioceses in the doldrums. But the damage is done, and the bland but insistent concerns of the institutions they serve eventually take precedence over the outrageousness of the Lord they once trusted and reveled in. They may start out busing tables and making fun of the institution every chance they get, but they end up as Club Stewards kowtowing to the Membership and living in fear of the Board of Directors.

Still, true as that sad story may be, it won't do for us to stigmatize such preachers and let it go at that. The church's consistent thrusting of ever larger stumbling blocks in front of the clergy's faith in Jesus Christ and him crucified can't just be tarred and feathered. The obstacles themselves need to be examined and understood if our dander against them is to do us any good. And since that's the job I propose for us in this chapter, let's get on with it.

I've already named what I consider to be the great-grandfather of all stumbling blocks: the fear of *losing* — of looking like a failure, and above all of *being* a failure. On examination, however, it turns out to be an odd fear. For one thing, it's clean contrary to the words of Jesus: "Those who save their life will lose it, and those who lose their life for my sake will save it." That passage from the ninth chapter of Luke comes right after Jesus' first prediction of his death and right before his transfiguration, when Moses and Elijah speak to him about his ἔξοδος, his *going out* into death. And those events occur immediately prior to the beginning of his final journey to Jerusalem and Good Friday. If that Friday, as we claim to believe, is the best thing that ever happened to the world — if we have been rescued by the world's champion Loser — it's got to be surpassing strange that we're afraid of the very failures that are our personal sacraments of salvation.

But there's something even more strange about our fear. Anybody who gives even a moment's attention to the way human life usually runs (namely, downhill) can spot what it is. It's the sheer *inexorability* of our losing. Climb as high as we may on the ladder of success, we progressively lose our grip. We start out healthy and end up sick. (Some of us start out sick and end up sicker.) We start out in possession (more or less) of our faculties and end up losing our marbles (or at least some of them). But above all, we start out alive and end up dead. Dead poor sometimes, or dead drunk, or dead tired, or dead in our sins — but always and without fail, just plain dead.

Nevertheless, far from being bad news, that inevitability of death turns out to be the best news the world has ever heard — and not only as far as the Gospel is concerned. Even the "natural" world (the "old" creation) runs by death. Death has always been the engine of life: every living thing flourishes by the forfeiture of other lives. The robin eats the worm, the cat eats the robin, the fox eats the cat — and the fox, once expired, is eaten by the worm's grandchildren: nothing can survive by trying to digest pebbles. What the Gospel assures us of, therefore, is that the New Creation runs the same way: "Greater love has no one than this, that he lay down his life for his friends" (John 15:13). The expiration of one creature is what makes the respiration of other creatures possible. How peculiar it is, then, that we spend our lives in a frenzy of fearing death as if it were suffocation! We avoid it like the plague whenever we ourselves can, but then we turn around and furiously inflict it on our fellow creatures all over the map. The human race frantically tries to convince itself of its right to go on breathing forever; but then, in the furtherance of that conviction, it resolutely chokes off creature after creature by means of wars, pogroms, and the death penalty — and strangles species after species by ecological arrogance.

The story of the fall of Adam and Eve in the third chapter of Genesis is instructive here. Daniel Quinn, in his novel *Ishmael*, makes a fascinating suggestion about what the Tree of the Knowledge of Good and Evil says about the nature of human sin. (I take the liberty of paraphrasing him, but I think I do him justice.)

When our first parents ate of the fruit of that tree, they were not doing a merely bad act — a single, deadly sin that would get them in Dutch with God. The serpent in the garden had bigger plans. He was tempting them to the same thing the devil in the wilderness tempted Jesus to: not the commission of specific wrongs but the complete subversion *of God's management of the world*. In suggesting that they eat of the fruit of the Tree of the Knowledge of *Good and Evil*, he was trying to get them to steal God's knowledge of the clever and delicate balance between good and evil — the knowledge by which he alone decides *who will live and who will die* — and relocate it permanently inside their own heads. *"God knows,"* the Adversary told them, *"that when you eat of it your eyes will be opened and you will be like God, knowing* [that is, able to manage all by yourselves] *good and evil* [that is, the determination of who lives and who dies]."

Now if we flip that interpretation of the story into a twentieth-century chronology of the universe, we get an interesting result. First of all, since God's management of life on earth seems to date from the primeval ooze about 50 billion years ago — and since his knowledge of what would live and what would die seems to have been adequate enough, in its hands-off policy, to make evolution go swimmingly — it would appear that there was no need for his creatures to bother their heads (if any) with such knowledge. But second, since *human* life (depending on how you define it) began anywhere from 3 million to 50 thousand years ago — and since human beings, for all of that time, seem to have evolved just as nicely — it would appear that even they didn't try to usurp the divine management-style, *at first*. There seems to have been a nice balance for a while (even a time of *innocence*, if you please) — at least until we upset the apple cart of creation by our adversarial management.

But now comes the interesting question: Where, on the evolutionary timeline, does that put Adam, Eve, and the Serpent? Well, since the earliest appearance of the human race's management-compulsion seems to have occurred around 8,000 B.C. (with the advent of agriculture in the Fertile Crescent), let's settle for that date. As corroboration for that speculation, Quinn adduces the story of the murder of Abel by Cain in Genesis 4 — Abel being one of the old, pre-agricultural good guys (the hands-off nomadic shepherd), and Cain being the hands-on villain (the sod-busting farmer). He also suggests that God's parting shot to their father, Adam, on the way out of Eden in the previous chapter ("Cursed is the ground because of you; in toil you shall eat of it . . . thorns and thistles it shall bring forth . . . by the sweat of your face you shall eat bread until you return to the ground"; NRSV) is not so much the punishment for a wicked act as it is a simple prediction of the carnival of chaos that will result from Adam's and Eve's takeover of the management of creation.

What Quinn doesn't mention, however, is the clincher. There were *two* trees of sacramental significance in Eden. At the very end of the story in Genesis 3, when God throws Adam and Eve out of the old, laissez-faire garden of their flourishing ("of *all* the trees you may eat *except* . . ."), he sets up a flaming sword to "guard the

18

way to the Tree of *Life*." He condemns them to death, you see, because if they were to live forever as the ultimate arbiters of who lives and who dies, *the whole world would die* — which, under our 10,000 years of disastrous arbitration, it seems very soon and suitably about to do.

But all is by no means lost. This detour through the Garden of Eden has served nicely to enable us to advance the argument of this book to the point of naming the biggest obstacle to the faith of preachers: their unwillingness to accept death as *the instrument of their personal salvation*. I think it was an early Christian writer who had the boldness to call the sentence of death pronounced on Adam in Genesis the "first proclamation of the Gospel" — of the *Good* News that our death, in and by Jesus' death, will be our salvation. Even our death in sin. God will indeed take back the management of creation. But he will take it back only as he took it on in the first place: by *letting things be,* even by *letting our sins be.* With nails through his hands and feet, at three o'clock on a dark Friday afternoon, he will die our now unmanageable death, take our disastrous knowledge of good and evil down into the darkness of his dead human mind, and by refusing to play God by our rules, he will restore our freedom to be human again in the silence of Jesus' tomb. All we can do, or need to do, is *trust* him.

FOUR

The Biggest Obstacle

I detect a narrowing of your eyes. You feel, I suspect, that I ought to apologize for the cheerfulness of my rhapsodies on death in the last chapter. But I won't. I believe Jesus has made death the biggest break we're ever going to get. Anyway, I'm still squarely on the subject of the preacher's *faith*. And I've now given you enough background to enable us to talk about the major obstacle to it: our dread of being branded as losers because of our *sins* — and above all, our fear of admitting to ourselves that we're nothing but what Ephesians 2:1 says we are: "*dead* in our trespasses and sins."

If death is the engine of life (and if lastness, lostness, leastness, and littleness are the only keys that can start that engine for us before death itself), then the *sins* of preachers — the *naughtinesses* for which they are despised and set at naught — are the choicest keys they have to the authentic preaching of life out of death by the Passion of Jesus. Unless we who speak the Word are willing to be utterly nothing — unless we're willing to admit we're sinners, and welcome the annihilation of our glittering images of moral success and clerical reputability — our words will be nothing more than the words of fakers, and we'll never come within a million miles of that astonishment at grace which alone can make those words come alive. We must not despise our sins, or fear them as evidence of condemnation; we must *relish* them as the most impressive testimonials we have to our salvation. That may strike you

20

as illegal and immoral, if not irresponsibly fattening; but better people than you or I have said it before: *O felix culpa!* O happy fault!

> Amazing grace! how sweet the sound,
> that saved a wretch like me!
> I once was lost, but now am found,
> was blind, but now I see.

We may love to sing the tune to John Newton's hymn, but in our heart of hearts we find its words a little too "eighteenth-century" for our sensibilities, a bit *overwrought* for our twentieth-century tastes. Why? Because our minds are caught over two very different barrels. On the one hand, we spend our lives trying to convince ourselves that we're *nice* people — not blameworthy characters, and certainly not the dead ducks that Scripture tells us we are. Liturgically, of course, we admit that we're sinners. But when the time comes that we've done something undeniably (and above all, unconcealably) rotten, what do we do? We go into a paroxysm of *guilt* over it. Or, if we have the chutzpah to avoid that trap, we walk the other way and psychologize it into a *sickness* — thus disclaiming personal ownership of the very death in which we are saved. We finagle ourselves into thinking we're the *victims* of our failures, not the *perpetrators of* them. But since even victims can't shake the notion of guilt entirely, we keep on walking the other way till we find somebody else to blame: we resort to the now fashionable device of confronting the parents (or whoever) who *victimized* us. Thus we arrive at the ultimate deprivation: we rob ourselves of the ability to celebrate the grace that meets us *in* our sins, not *after* them. "While we were still sinners, Christ died for us" (Rom. 5:8) — not just when and if we get around to repenting. John Newton rejoiced over the lostness in which he met grace. We think it would have been healthier for all of us if he could have gotten off the wretchedness kick and revved up the power of positive blaming.

On the other hand, when a notable sin does catch up with us

— when it becomes publicly and painfully clear that in some instant, disastrous case we have done something that unflinchingly proclaims us *no damn good* — we feel (and we're frequently told in no uncertain terms) that we have *no right to preach*. We collapse in an orgy of useless guilt. Please note that. Guilt is supremely useless — and unscriptural to boot. There is no word in the New Testament that corresponds to what we now mean by it. There are, to be sure, words for "guilty": there's ἔνοχος, meaning "liable for" or "subject to"; there's ὀφείλειν, meaning "to owe"; and there's ὑπόδικος, meaning "under the power of the judicial system." But those are all about legal guilt, not the precious psychological hang-up we know and love so well.

Our fascination with guilt is a blind alley (especially for preachers) because the New Testament isn't about guilt at all; it's about forgiveness. The Lamb of God has *taken away* the sins of the world, not laid them on us like a coat of tar. Furthermore, we celebrate that absolution every Sunday in the Nicene Creed: "We acknowledge one baptism for the forgiveness of sins." Notice what a remarkable statement that is: it proclaims that by the grace of God, we live all our lives in an *irremovable suit of forgiveness*. It tells us that every sin we ever commit will be committed *inside* that suit — and therefore that every sin in our lives is forgiven before, during, and after our commission of it. We don't need to *get* forgiveness; we need to learn how to *cheer up* in the forgiveness we've had all along. "There is therefore now no condemnation for those who are in Christ Jesus" (Rom. 8:1; NRSV).

Of course there must be repentance. But even repentance is a celebration, not a bargaining session in which we work up enough resolve against sin to con God into putting up with us. It's not a turning from sin but a return to faith — a reawakening of our trust that *all* our deeds, bad as well as good, have been *done in God* (see John 3:21). God doesn't run away from our sins or from the sins of any human being; he meets us in them by the indwelling of his incarnate Word in every last child of Adam and Eve. And thus, since even our sins were done in the Light that is Jesus, all we have to do about them is *the truth* (John 3:21, again). We don't have to feel guilty about them. We don't even have to overcome them (which, in any case, is more than we could realistically promise). We have only to admit them — to *own* them as they are in the truth of our condition, and to *celebrate* them as the death in which grace gives us life. *"O felix culpa"* one more time. "Amazing grace!"

Alas, in the present panic over faddish clerical derelictions, the church can't see that for beans. Bad enough that its preachers think their sins make them unfit to preach forgiveness. Worse yet by far that the church itself — for the dreadful reason that it might have the shirt sued off its corporate back if it keeps an avowed homosexual or a known adulterer in the pulpit — chases offending preachers unceremoniously (and with precious little due process) off the farm. Don't interrupt me; I'm on a roll here. I refuse to be distracted by arguments from the right (with which I happen to disagree) that homosexual acts are always and everywhere sinful — or by noises from the left (with which I happen to agree) that predatory behavior is profoundly wrong. So are a host of other clerical offenses, and we don't make *them* impediments to ordination or grounds for dismissal. We who are ordained have always had our fair share of the world's liars, louts, and closet letches — not to mention our cadres of boozers, backbiters, and bores. My only point is this: in the current fuss over sexual harassment, the church is losing its grip on the Gospel of grace in the quagmire of the notion that it's God's moral cop on the beat.

If a sinner can't proclaim forgiveness, who's left to preach? Who, for that matter, could preach better, or with more passion? Of all the deaths that are available to us before we're stone-cold dead, our death in sin is the most embarrassingly *convincing* share in the Passion most of us will ever have. The church is not in the world to teach sinners how to straighten up and fly right. That's the world's business; and on the whole it does a fairly competent — even a gleefully aggressive — job of it. The church is supposed to be in the forgiveness business. Its job in filling pulpits is to find derelict nobodies who are willing to admit that they're sinners and

23

mean it. It's supposed to take sheep who can be nothing but lost — sons who can accept their failure as sons, crooked tax collectors who can stare at their shoes and say they're worthless human beings — and stand them up to proclaim that lostness, deadness, uselessness, and nothingness are God's cup of tea. The church's job is not to go around implying that those desperate states are conditions we must get over as quickly as possible once we've been found; its true work is to invite us all to go moonstruck over the news that the one operative consideration in our life is the *Passion of the Finder to find* — the wild enthusiasm of the God who makes all things, old and new, by bringing them out of nothing but *nothing*.

Out of nothing. *Ex nihilo.* Out of 100 percent, 24-karat non-existence. Not out of nothing as a *precondition* of being, but nothing as the *matrix* of being from start to finish. One of the worst things that ever happened to the church was the importation into its doctrinal structure of the Greek notion of the immortality of the human soul. Because do you know what that did? It persuaded us that nothingness is something that God has no serious use for anymore. Once the church had enticed us with the notion of a finer, more spiritual part of our nature — a beautiful butterfly of a soul which, once it is released from the nasty cocoon of the body, will shoot up to heaven by its own rocketry — we convinced ourselves that *we would never have to be nothing again.* Which gave us a mere half-reason for needing Jesus as our resurrection: we would never be more than half dead. We turned Jesus into a kind of celestial mechanic who would bolt repaired bodies back onto souls that had made it to the heavenly garage on their own. The Protestants among us refused to talk about the soul after death, and the Roman Catholics got the bright idea of running the soul through the car wash of purgatory before the Last Day. All of us were agreed, though, that there would never be a time when we were truly dead — when we had gone all the way back into the nothing from which we came.

Worse yet, that denial of our eventual nothingness was only half of a bad bargain. We also forgot that we're nothing *right now* —

24

that we come into being out of nothing at every moment of our existence. We live all our lives knee-deep, up to our eyebrows, and totally over our heads in it. And we are brought out of that nothing *twice*. When I urge people to chuck the immortality of the soul as a piece of anti-Gospel baggage, they worry. They tell me, "Look, this is 1997. What about 2097? If I don't have an immortal soul, and the Rapture doesn't happen in the meantime, where will I be then?" I tell them, "*You* look: what are you worried about? You were nothing in 1797, and it hasn't bothered you so far. Why should it bother you now? Can't God do the same trick a second time? Hasn't he promised to do exactly that? Besides, you've already been told that you're dead and risen right now. At your baptism, you were assured that in its waters you were 'buried with Christ in his death' then and there. Therefore, you've been dead since you were born: Death and death alone — nothing and nothing alone — has always been what's given you life. *'The hour is coming and now is,'* Jesus says in John 5:25, *'when the dead* [not the living, or the half-dead] *will hear the voice of the Son of God and live.'* Jesus came to raise the dead. Not to repair the repairable, correct the correctable, or improve the improvable. Just to raise the dead, and nobody but the dead. Nothing is all he needs for anything."

Let me give you an analogy. We tend to think of God's creation and redemption of the world as two separate acts; but for him they're inseparable aspects of one single act. To see that, picture an LPGA golfer — a woman at the top of her form, standing on the tee. After her backswing, when she has the driver poised motionless behind her head, nothing is happening: that's the *moment before* the moment of creation. Then she swings the club down and strikes the ball: that's the *moment of creation* itself. But then comes the follow-through: that's the *moment of redemption*. If its indispensable influence on the ball isn't already in the works at the top of her backswing (that is, in the *nothing* before the *something*), then the *something* (the ball — or in God's case, the creation) won't fly right. So she has to have both creation and redemption — both her hands-on striking of the ball *into* freedom and her hands-off guidance of the ball *in* its freedom — built in right from the start. By one swing, she strikes the ball *out of nothing* and corrects its course *by nothing* to a hole in one.

If that's true of God and the golfer, it's true to the nth degree for the sinner who gets up to preach. Listen to Paul, "the chief of sinners," in 1 Corinthians 1:27: "God purposely chose what the world considers nonsense in order to shame the wise, and he chose what the world considers weak in order to shame the powerful. He chose what the world looks down on and despises and thinks is *nothing* [τὰ μὴ ὄντα] in order to destroy what the world thinks *exists* [τὰ ὄντα]." All God needs to make a universe is nothing; all he needs to make a preacher is a nobody. And the closest preachers ever come in this life to that most usable of all conditions is getting caught *in flagrante delicto* and being told they're bums.

Let me bear a little personal witness here. Almost from the start of my life as a priest, I was a pretty good preacher — as preachers go. I was also a born teacher and a demon explainer (though I seldom knew when to shut up and let people figure things out for themselves — but then, nobody's perfect). But I never quite got around to being a passionate enthusiast over what God had done for me personally in Jesus. Why? Well, I now think it was because I believed, back then, that I wasn't broken enough to need fixing. But some twenty years ago, after a long love affair (twenty-four years!), I committed the unpardonable romantic sin of infidelity to the beloved, and made the monumentally stupid mistake of confessing it to the beloved herself — all in an unshakable assurance that I could repent so persuasively that she'd have to forgive me. (At the time, that was the sum and substance of my idea of repentance: a negotiation in which I was certain that my sincerity would give me the upper hand.)

But it didn't. And in the course of one lunch at an Italian restaurant, the love that had been my life went galley-west for good: twenty-four years of wine, roses, poetry, and passion went whistling down the wind. My first reaction, of course, was denial: it just couldn't be happening. My second reaction, though, was anger: she *had* to forgive me, dammit! (I won't even bother you with my other reactions because they're beside the point. One way or another, they were every last one of them attempts to get back what I thought of as my *control* over the situation — to get my life back to where I felt it belonged, namely, with me in the driver's seat.)

Suffice it to say I went on that way for almost a year. But then it slowly began to dawn on me that my control wasn't going to come back: I was going to have to face something I'd never seriously faced before: the fact that I was *powerless*. None of the devices I tried to use on her did any good. My control hadn't slipped; it was gone. But in the end — and with me fighting the realization every inch of the way — the truth came to me: it wasn't that I was powerless, or out of control, or unhappy, or hurt. I was *dead*. I had no more influence than a corpse over my own life.

No doubt you find that even more overwrought than "Amazing grace!" You want to say to me, "Really, now! You must have led a very sheltered life. Lots of people have love affairs blow up in their faces; but they get up and brush themselves off without having to exalt the experience into a bush-league death. Your problem wasn't powerlessness; it's just that you were spoiled."

Well . . . , I grant you that. I *was* spoiled; and it was a distinctly bush-league death. But it was the first death I'd ever had, and it was enough for God to get me to welcome the Passion into my life. So if God doesn't balk at the quality of anyone's death (the church's 2,000-year-long fuss over suicides notwithstanding), you shouldn't balk at mine. Besides, it was *my* death. I, who had spent fifty years trying to convince everybody (myself included) that I was *something else*, had ended up as nothing whatsoever. Not as guilty, or as a sinner, or as a basket case; but as a zero. Yet suddenly, by the grace of God, every light in the New Testament went on, and everything that the church had in her basement of belief hit me like cask-strength, single-malt Scotch: *This was where I had been all along!* I didn't have to get over my death; I had only to be *in it* — because that was where Jesus my life was. I developed, in short, a passion for the Passion.

And a passion for the resurrection in my death as well, because Jesus my resurrection is there too. My preaching improved, I think. I even made a (modest) buck out of being dead and risen, because when I figured out that Jesus had always held me that way, I was able to put my thoughts about it down on paper and get them published. So if you want to tell me my resurrection was as bush-league as my death, be my guest. You can't insult a corpse. I'm nothing; Jesus is everything.

Eventually, we're going to talk about the practicalities of preaching in this book — preparation, outlines, notes, all that. But first let me tell you about a gambit for the moments immediately before preaching I recently came upon. After a week of refining my notes (I never did write out my sermons), and after making a fair copy of them at 4:00 on Sunday morning, and after highlighting them before the first service and drawing arrows all over them in the sacristy to improve their logic, I arrive in the pulpit during the hymn before the Gospel — and I don't sing the hymn, or even take one last peek at my notes. I just go as blank as I can. I try to put my overactive mind as near to nothing as I can get it. I imagine myself as a corpse, or a hollow skin, or an empty vessel. And I hold on to that image: that's what I am, and that's all I am. It's too late now for me to be somebody or to do something: *if Jesus has anything he wants me to say, he'll have to arrange for it himself.* And since I'm about to sign myself with the cross three times before the Gospel, I say inwardly, "Jesus my Lover, Jesus my Love, Jesus my Death and my Life." Then I announce the Gospel, and at the end of it — just hoping he finds a use for me — I preach. You could do worse.

For in the end nothing counts, and nothing *alone* counts, in the drawing of his Love and the voice of his Calling. Even your *faith* doesn't matter. I mean that. Your faith may make a difference to *you* — to your enjoyment of the divine comedy you're selling tickets to, and to the hilarity of your pitches for it. But it doesn't matter to God. He's assured you that he's brought the scenario of creation and redemption to its conclusion *all by himself,* without assistance from you or anybody. You may believe him or not believe him. You may trust him on Monday, Wednesday, and Friday, and decide he's full of baloney on Tuesday, Thursday, and Saturday. And on Sunday, you may proclaim your faith in him, or prattle on about your erudition, or indulge your talent for quoting second-rate poetry. Or you can call in sick. But none of it will hold even an unlit candle to what he has done for you.

Jesus himself said as much in Matthew 25 — in the last of his formal utterances before his Passion: the parable of The Sheep and the Goats at the Last Judgment. We habitually read that scene as a warning that if we're not like the blessed sheep who ministered to the Shepherd/King in the least of his brethren, we'll end up in everlasting fire like the cursed goats. But I don't think we can make that stick: Jesus purposely sets up the parable to preclude such a moralistic interpretation. We can't make moral theology out of it because there's no morality in it: neither the sheep nor the goats had the slightest clue that they were dealing (or not dealing) with the King: there are no grounds for the blame dished out! What I think Jesus was up to in The Sheep and the Goats was the same thing he had in mind in Matthew 22, in The King's Son's Wedding. When Jesus had the King murder all the first-invited guests who refused to show up at his son's wedding, he was using his talent for parabolic mayhem to get the concept of *deserving* out of the story. Here, he's using his talent for wide-angle condemnation to get the notion of *morality* — and in particular, the notion that your faith is some sweaty and rewardable work, without which God refuses to save you — out of the parable.

Think about that. In the two previous parables in chapter 25 of Matthew (the Ten Virgins and the Talents), Jesus has said that only unvarnished faith — with no coats of works whatsoever — will matter at the Last Day. But since we're such experts at turning even faith into a work (since we pride ourselves on thinking there must be at least something we can do to give the divine Rescuer a helping hand), he does a dramatic about-face in this parable: he says that even our faith has nothing to do with the success of the divine plan. (Remember? Jesus is just a day or two away from the cross — from the death by which he will *do it all*.) He states flatly that everybody, with no exceptions, will find him nowhere but in the brokenness of the world: in the last, the lost, the least, the little, and the dead. There, and nowhere else, is where he works to save. But then what does he do? Well, in chapter 26, Matthew shows him heading straight down the chute into his Passion. He is broken, and he dies. He takes up permanent residence in the shipwreck of the world. He makes all the disasters of our history the sacraments of his saving presence.

Perhaps you feel I'm forcing the parable. You may be accustomed to thinking of Jesus' parables as lessons in loveliness, as bits of advice to *us*. If so, you fail to see what in fact they are: *autobiographical sketches of the way God in Christ works*. They're about the Kingdom of God first and foremost, not about us. They're about the fact that he does everything that needs doing, and that his overriding judgment on everybody — the κρίσις he brings to the lives of all — is a crisis of *approval*, not condemnation. He is going to be lifted up on the cross and draw all to himself out of the nothing of their deaths. His last word to us, as he holds us in his death (our sins included), will be that we're just fine by his Father. The first word at the final judgment will always be "You're okay!"

That's why I think my interpretation stands up: if Jesus is going to draw *all* to himself, why would he — at this last, crucial juncture — go out of his way to give us reasons to think he's going to draw *some*? After all, the sheep and the goats alike were his. He was as much in the inevitable brokenness of both as he was in the brokenness of the hungry, the thirsty, the sick, and the imprisoned to whom they did or didn't minister. Whether they worked or shirked, therefore — whether they believed or disbelieved — his presence in them and to them in their death was all the heaven there ever was. Try as they may or rebel as they might, they could never manage to get out of it.

Hell, it goes without saying, is presented as an option in this parable. It's an odd option, however: it has *no existential referent*. You can indeed "go to hell"; but the only place you can go there from is heaven. And even that's a pretty thin possibility, since once you're dead, you can't get out of a heaven that's run solely on the basis of raising the dead. You don't get there on your own steam; you get there after you've run out of steam and there's nothing left to move you anywhere but the eternal suction of a resurrection that draws everything out of nothing.

If you like, you may refuse to believe you've been drawn into the eternal party. You can't stop the party, though. You may try, if you like, to walk out on it and look for another bar to drown your sorrows in. But it's the loneliest walk in the universe: there is no other bar, and when you get done with all your walking, you'll find you went nowhere. Jesus does seem to insist that we're capable of being stupid enough to try and stay in that hell forever — and that God will even go so far as to utter a frustrated Lover's "Oh, damn!" over our stupidity. I'm not about to argue with that. Yet even if it's the Gospel truth, all of your hell will be *at the party,* sequestered in the nail print in the left hand of the Bridegroom at the Supper of the Lamb. To say it one last time: even your faith doesn't matter, except to your own enjoyment of what he does for you. You can trust or not trust, but it doesn't change his mind or alter the facts. As far as he's concerned, you're home free forever. That's the deal. It would be a good idea just to shut up and accept it.

FIVE

Grim Pills

I know. If you're a preacher, you have a sneaking suspicion that I'm deliberately provoking you. Back at the beginning of Chapter Three, when I characterized your congregation as addicted to religion pills, spirituality pills, and morality pills, you may have felt a twinge of fondness for me as a possible help to your preaching. But since then, especially after my hymns to nothingness and my praise of nobodies, you're not so sure. My insistence that guilt is useless, that God saves us in death and not by religion, and that my own sins were happy faults — not to mention my alarming assertion that even our faith makes no difference to the sovereignty of the grace of God — is beginning to make you wonder if I'm not more of a menace than a help.

My response to you is that I'm afraid I have to be both: I'm convinced I can't be a help without being a menace first. Addiction is like that — as you know perfectly well from having done counseling yourself (or from being counseled), if not from having let an AA group use your parish house and hung around long enough to get the general drift of "tough love." Let me say it straight out. I think the reason why there's so much poor preaching in the church is that preachers, by and large, are as addicted to religion as their congregations are. I don't exclude myself, either. I can invent a new religion (or lapse back into an old one) as fast as the next Christian. We're all druggies. We slip into the stupor of imagining there are

32

things we *have to do* — some additive of religious works we have to put into the gasoline of grace — if the gift of God is to get its work done in us. And the sad thing about it is that we'll scour the New Testament (especially the Epistles, and in particular the Pastoral Epistles) for every moral "requirement" and religious "condition" we can find in order to slap a behavioral surcharge on our free acceptance in the Beloved. So in the interests of fairness to your congregation, I have to give you an equally hard time.

Still, I do owe you a little more clarity about why I call religion, spirituality, and morality "grim pills." We're so convinced that they're unqualifiedly respectable subjects that it won't do to castigate them by title and let it go at that. Hence this essay on their dangers.

To begin with, they're nothing more than three packagings of the same pain-killer. Or, better said, religion is the generic version of the drug, while spirituality and morality are the higher-priced name brands. Moreover, the pain we take them to kill is the agony of not having *control* over our lives. The ostensible purpose of religion is to give us the power to make things happen the way they "should"; but all it gives us is the *illusion* of such control. We swallow it in the same hope with which Adam and Eve ate the fruit of the Tree of the Knowledge of Good and Evil: to convince ourselves that when all is said and done, *we're* the ones in charge of the management of creation. That never works. We may think that we're practicing our religion because God told us to. But the side effect of the drug is always and invariably the depressing feeling that if we don't practice it, God either won't be able to help us, or he'll get mad and decide not to (which amounts to the same thing). And all that, in spite of the fact that in Jesus, he's flatly announced that there's not a single religious thing we need to do. On the cross, he has made "by the one oblation of himself once offered, a full, perfect, and sufficient sacrifice, oblation, and satisfaction for the sins of the whole world." That quote from the old Anglican canon of the Eucharist uses "religious" words to proclaim the *end of religion* in Jesus. It's over. The drugstore is closed. The free gift of grace — without a single pious response — is all that counts.

Furthermore, it doesn't make any difference if you take the exalted view that at least some religious requirements (the sacrifices of the Old Covenant, for example, or the prohibition of homosexual acts) have been enjoined by God himself. Because in the New Testament (in which, as Christians believe, God reveals what he's been up to *all along*), he becomes incarnate in a Person of remarkably cavalier attitudes toward religion. Jesus eats and drinks with sinners; he is tried for the capital crime of blasphemy; he dies under the curse of the religious law; and he then has the effrontery to insist that whatever it was that religion had been trying (and failing) to do has been done once and for all by that festival of irreligion. Not only that, but he eventually arranges for the author of the Epistle to the Hebrews to show up and say that even a revealed religion couldn't do the job: "It is impossible for the blood of bulls and goats to take away sins" (10:4; NRSV). All those old priests and sacrifices, all those fulminations against sin, were a come-on for the day when he would declare the entire enterprise bankrupt and get out of the religion racket for good.

Moreover, it makes even less difference if your religion of choice is a fine, uplifting enterprise like spirituality or sanctification — or a mere superstition like the church-growth movement, seeker-oriented approaches to piety, prayer walks, inner harmony, or not stepping on sidewalk cracks. All those enthusiasms are what Jesus called "tithing mint, anise, and cummin" (KJV): they trick you into living by coming up to pharisaic scratch rather than by lying low in Jesus' death. None of them gives you the least relief from the pain of being out of control because none of them controls anything — or comes within even a light year of the Good News you're supposed to be preaching. Nevertheless, you probably still object. Deep down, you're beginning to think my contention that religion is a drug makes me a menace not just to you but to God, to Scripture, and to the church. Let me change the metaphor, therefore, from substance abuse to *war* for a few paragraphs and see if that helps.

War is an attempt to seize, defend, and control the management of the world; religion is the same thing. Or, more accurately, religion is our attempt to seize the management of history and to defend our usurpation of it *in order to control* creation. To go back to Daniel Quinn and put it in his terms, religion is an activity of the "takers" — of those who, like Cain, have to put their blood-soaked hands all over the world — rather than of the "leavers" who can let it be its own divinely permitted self. Before the Fall, Adam and Eve were "leavers": they didn't seize, defend, or control the garden of the world; they just owned up to their modestly magnificent place in it, and they tended it and delighted in it. To be sure, "leaver" elements are still evident in the religions of native peoples — and they're admirable. But those aren't the religions I'm talking about. What I have in mind here is the "taking" compulsion that's preoccupied the Judeo-Christian tradition almost from the start, and which has been unqualified bad news throughout the rest of its history. Look at the evidence.

In the architecture of the book of Genesis, it's quite plain that the human race's urge to seize, defend, and control the world by means of religion popped into history immediately after the Fall. The first, murderous argument between Cain and Abel was a religious one: a fight over whose sacrifice was the more acceptable to God. Furthermore, the Flood is portrayed as a punishment for sin, Noah builds an altar after it's over and offers burnt offerings, and the Tower of Babel story is presented as evidence of a desire to make human management reach to the heavens.

But I want to push the subject back even further and say that the invention of religion *was* the Fall — or that the Fall was *itself* the invention of religion, whichever way you want to put it. As I've said, what Adam and Eve did in the garden was to jury-rig an essentially religious system for getting the management of good and evil out of God's hands and into theirs. They seized, defended, and controlled a territory that God was handling quite nicely on his own. The precise wrong in their snatching was not that they found the tree "good for food" or a "delight to the eyes." (Those were simply perceptions of the goodness of all creation, the ill-fated Tree of Management included.) Their *sin* lay in the discovery of something which wasn't there at all and which was never in God's cards — something of no creative use whatsoever. What they came up with was the dim idea that the tree was to be desired *to make them wise*. Having embarked on their campaign to conquer history for themselves, they inevitably found that it could never bring them victory in the real world, only in the world of religion. They concocted, in short, a *parallel universe* inside their own heads — and then, with the weapons of their own wisdom, they invoked that universe in the midst of this one and started a *war* against reality.

Let me go back now to the pills and see if I can convince you of their grimness. It's a commonplace that religion has three constituent elements: *cult, creed,* and *conduct. Cult* is all the ceremonial rigmarole (like Noah's burnt offerings) that you have to go through in order to persuade God to continue being pleasant to you. It's the *generic substance* itself, religion *qua* religion: sacrifices for sin, nights of prayer, days of fasting, and whole seasons of beating up on yourself. *Creed* is all the things you have to think correctly about in order to be religious. It's the *intellectual* name-brand of the drug: the doctrines you have to believe and the heresies you have to extirpate. And to end the list, *conduct* is the *behavioral* name-brand. It's the struggle to comply with long lists of spiritual or ethical requirements you have to fulfill if you want to be on God's good side. It's either the struggle to achieve secure possession of godliness, inner peace, white-hot devotion, and industrial-strength unworldliness; or else it's the total avoidance of ethical missteps like being a liar, a cheat, a thief, or someone who goes to bed with her brother.

Since that probably sounds flippant to you, let me hasten to add the one kind word that can unpatronizingly be said about religion. It does have a redeeming feature: it's the human race's historic witness to our awareness that something is seriously out of whack with the way we try to manage life. Even though I've said that religion is the biggest management error of all time — and despite the fact that it commands us to do all kinds of things we would never have bothered with if we hadn't invented religion in the first place (there was no religion in Eden when it was under

36

God's management) — it stands as a testimony to the fact that we owe both God and our neighbors an apology for making the world such a mess. In short, religion reminds us that we're damaged goods. Having given it that much credit, though, it's still a loser: after 10,000 years of religion, the world is not noticeably a better place. Indeed, under our religious manipulations, it's gotten decidedly worse. Here, therefore, ends the kind word. Time for three short excursions into cult, creed, and conduct.

Cult. It doesn't work. In the earlier parts of the Bible, God seems to be convinced it might. (See the instructions for worshipping in the Tabernacle in Exodus 26 to 30, or the rite for the healing of a leper in Leviticus 13 and 14.) But later on, he seems to have thought better (actually, worse) of the subject. He sends the prophet Micah, for example, to convey his increasingly dim view of it: "Will the LORD be pleased with thousands of rams, or with ten thousands of rivers of oil?" (6:7). He sends his only begotten Son to go around breaking the Sabbath (see the four Gospels, throughout). He sends Paul to take potshots at the Law (see Romans and Galatians). He sends the letter to the Hebrews to say that *cult* is a wipe-out (see Hebrews 10). And in the end, he brings the New Jerusalem down from heaven with no Temple at all (Rev. 21:22). In a word, God reneges on religion.

Since the practices of religion never achieved even a scrap of what they promised, God just ignored them and won the game unscrupulously — by the irreligious device of dying as a common criminal. There is therefore now not only no condemnation for those who are in Christ Jesus; there isn't a single, *properly effective* religious act anywhere in the world, not even in the so-called Christian religion. We pray the *Lord's* Prayer, not our own. We fast to remind ourselves of *his* leastness, not our own heroics. In Baptism and the Eucharist, in Confession and Absolution, and in all the priestly acts of the church, we're celebrating what Jesus has already done, not negotiating with God to get him to do it.

Creed. Not only doesn't it work; it ends up working mischief. Religion as creed is another human effort at control. Our insistence that God will smile on us if we get our doctrines right and our theology up to snuff is nothing but a human head-trip. Far from making our management of the world run more smoothly, it's been one of our principal contributions to history's dangerous ride. Telling people what they have to think is as precarious as it is pointless: half of them refuse to listen; the other half wind up sounding like parrots. Furthermore, we've been in that predicament for a long time. The Reformation may have had the grace to spot the uselessness of the cultic aspect of medieval religion, but it fell flat on its face when it came to the dangers of creed. In fact, it worsened the situation. The Reformers took the minimal creedal structure of the medieval church and infected it with the cancer of officially imposed *propositional theology*. Everybody (Roman Catholics included) was required to sign on the dotted line of long-winded "confessions of faith" designed to give the right answers to every possible theological poser — no matter how far out in left field those answers put the Gospel.

Fundamentalism is nothing but the latest and worst form of that "confessionalism" — our most recent attempt at control via conformity. Depressingly, it infects the religious left as well as the religious right. The fundamentalism of the right won't let you preach Christ crucified unless you believe that God made the world on a Sunday morning in 4,004 B.C. And the fundamentalism of the left won't let you preach the expulsion of Adam as the first proclamation of the Gospel unless you promise *not* to believe that Adam actually existed. The whole charade is madness: piddling conformities of that sort are the death of theology, not to mention preaching. We've concentrated so long on putting fences and signs around Scripture that we've lost the ability to play in it. No wonder our sermons, right or left (particularly what we're pleased to call our doctrinal sermons), are such irrelevancies.

Conduct. This is the hands-down prizewinner in the religion-as-conformity contest. From Adam and Eve's discovery of sexual shame (which elicited God's zinger, "Who told you you were naked?"); to the Middle Ages' gleeful romance with hell as the just reward of the wicked; to the Reformation's insistence on good behavior as a test of church membership; to excommunication as the church's favorite indoor sport — and right on down to our own earnest flaps over responsibility, accountability, and political correctness as the hallmarks of religious folk — we've hidden the Gospel of grace under a bushel of moral judgments. We've eclipsed forgiveness as the Good News and made *guilt* the touchstone of our relationships, with God and with everybody else. Our religion has convinced us that we must not do a whole raft of fun things we were once allowed to do ("of *every* tree in the garden you may freely eat; just trust me and leave that one alone") because God and the church will disown us if we act on them.

And all that, in spite of the facts: one, we've never stopped doing them; two, we're not about to; and three, God has given up waiting for us to do them and left the subject of our conduct behind him in the empty tomb ("he has wiped away the handwriting in ordinances that was against us, and he has taken it out from between us and himself, nailing it to the cross"; Col. 2:14).

Perhaps that's enough for the three stooges of religion. Their slapstick performances of cult, creed, and conduct must not be taken seriously: if you won't laugh at them, you'll end up crying over the enormity of the damage they do. Their antics boil down to one thing only. They encourage us to find our identity by force — by pounding on the heads and pulling on the noses of everybody we know (God included) until they knuckle under to our control. But our efforts at control don't work any better than the three stooges' do. They just keep us so busy doing religious pratfalls that we never discover our true identity, which remains what it always has been — Jesus our life in our death.

Think about control in the history of our lives. We start out as babies in charge of nothing whatsoever: everything is done to us or for us, nothing by us. But then come the "terrible twos," and we begin a lifetime of putting whatever arm we can on everybody we run into. Next come our teens, when we despise all control except our own. After that come our own offspring, whose helplessness tricks us into controlling them as we ourselves were once controlled. Then come *their* teens, in which we find ourselves out of control all over again (and after that, their adulthood, in which we're not even thanked for our pains but viewed as victimizers). And during all those years of trying to manage our lives, we lose control more and more until our death — when we have none at all. Yet all the while we go right on thinking that one more effort at muscling things and people into religious order will make our identities come up roses. It's a wonder God even puts up with us.

SIX

Antidotes

Still, he does put up with us. In his mercy, he shortcuts our entire sorry progress and cuts straight to the chase: he makes the simple fact of our death the key to our restoration. Not control by cultic body-English. Not control by creedal correctness. Not control by moral jawboning. Just by death. Just by losing control. Just by reducing to insignificance all the religious works we hoped would be the signs of our success at running this show. He does it by giving us no sign except the Sign of Jonah — namely, *his own death and resurrection in Jesus his Son*. But since I've said most of that already, let me give you a few reflections on Scripture in the hope that you'll be a little more persuaded of what I'm saying.

In the ninth chapter of John, Jesus sees a man who has been blind from birth sitting as a beggar. Jesus says nothing; and the man, not seeing him, asks nothing. The disciples have a question, however: "Who sinned," they ask, "this man or his parents, to make him be born blind like that?" (v. 2). They don't pity him. They don't even put a dime in his cup. They go straight to the category of *conduct* in the hope of getting a religious handle on him. But Jesus tells them, "It isn't a matter of sin. Neither this man nor his parents are responsible for his blindness. He's blind in order that the *works of God* [I read that as a reference to the Mystery of Christ by which the incarnate Word restores all things in their brokenness] *might be made manifest in him*" (v. 3). Jesus says, "*We*

41

[that is, you and I together, my disciple friends] *need to do the works of the one who sent me while it's day; because the night is coming in which no one will be able to work* [except the God who operates in the darkness of death]" (v. 4). And having said that, he states flatly, *"Whenever"* — the word is ὅταν, "as often as"; I read it here as "on all the occasions" of the Mystery of his presence in creation — *"Whenever I am in the world, I am the light of the world"* (v. 5).

Then Jesus spits on the ground, makes a little paste out of the dirt, puts it on the man's eyes, and — not saying a word to him, not even about getting his sight back — tells him to go wash in a pool. (I should probably do something with the name of the pool, *Siloam*, which means "Sent"; but I won't. I've got bigger fish to fry.)

Those fish are the *faith* of the blind man and his *freedom* in it, versus the religious *knowledge* of everybody else in the passage. The Pharisees, for example, *know* what's wrong with the man, and they know how it ought to be controlled. Especially when it comes to this Jesus character. The word they use — οἴδαμεν, "we know" — is frequently on their lips. "We *know* this man is a sinner" (v. 24); "We *know* that God spoke to Moses, but as for this fellow, we *don't know* where he's coming from" (v. 29). By contrast, the blind man's parents *know* that he's their son and that he was born blind, but they feel it's safer *not to know* how he now sees or who opened his eyes (vv. 20-21).

But through it all, the *faith* of the blind man grows and grows. In his freedom, he's even able to bait the Pharisees with their own religious certainties: "Why, this is amazing," he says to them. "You claim you don't know where he's coming from, and yet he opened my eyes? We *know* [there's the baiting] that God doesn't hear sinners; but if anyone is God-fearing and does his will, him he hears" (vv. 30-31). Yet the Pharisees are not free: they're slaves to defending the old territory of cult, creed, and conduct they've been trying to control all their lives long. They can't even face reality anymore: they won't believe that the man was born blind, or that he got his sight back, until they get corroboration from his parents. On the other hand, the blind man's faith is doing fine. True, he doesn't get around to saying "I believe" (πιστεύω) until the end of the story. But right from the beginning, he *acts* in faith: he goes and washes when Jesus tells him to; and from then on he keeps up a steady drumbeat of bantering resistance to the certainties of his prosecutors, daring them to write him off.

And at the end, he becomes even freer in his faith: he banters with Jesus himself. The passage in which he does so (vv. 35-38) is the most fascinating one in the episode. To appreciate it, you have to remember that he's never seen Jesus. From the time the blind man starts for the pool to almost the end of the story, his healer just isn't around: It's as if Jesus is going out of his way to insist that he deals with nobody but losers. When the man was a blind beggar (and an uncontested loser), Jesus was with him (silently) all the way. Jesus does speak to him when he tells him to wash; but the man is still blind at that juncture, and thus still a loser. But after he receives his sight — after he becomes a winner, a celebrity of sorts — Jesus leaves him on his own with nothing but his faith. It's a hint of the *absence of the God-character* that Jesus carefully inserts into each of his parables of judgment in Matthew 25 (the Ten Virgins, the Talents, and the Great Judgment) to underscore the *sole necessity of faith* when we come to the final reckoning. But let that pass too.

Once the man is again a full-fledged loser, however — when the Pharisees throw him out (v. 34) — Jesus returns. He finds the man, and he pops what sounds for all the world like an off-the-wall theological question to him: "Do you believe in the Son of Man?" (v. 35). It's as if he walked up to a stranger and asked, "Do you believe in the Rapture?" But the man is as sharp as he is steadfast: he says, "Who might that be, Sir [κύριε], that I might believe in him?" (v. 36). And Jesus says, "You've already seen him; he's the one who's talking to you" (v. 37). And then the blind man who has seen by faith all along delivers the punch line: "'I *believe* [πιστεύω], Sir'; [the word is κύριε again, but John intends it to be read now as *Lord*] — and he *worships him*" (v. 38).

As almost always happens in John, the story ends on the note of *believing*. In this case, the note struck is that of the *faith of losers* as opposed to the knowing of winners. It's about trust in the "absent God" — in the Mystery of the incarnate Lord who hides in the least and lowest, and who's the one Person who matters. Which means, in the case of those he chooses to preach that faith, that he wants empty vessels: preachers who have no religion left to preach and who are thus prime candidates for being shrugged off by a religion-besotted church. The church, of course, may legitimately employ the *forms* of religion, but that's only because it's proclaiming the fulfillment of the job that religion was trying (and failing) to do. Apart from that, what we're supposed to preach has nothing to do with religion.

One more proof text and we're ready to move along in this subject. In the ninth chapter of Acts, we have the story of the conversion of Saul on the road to Damascus. You know it perfectly well, but it's worth our while to examine its peculiarities. Saul was a Pharisee, an ardent religionist; and like all such, he had a consuming interest in rounding up heretics. He persecuted the church because religion was his identity — and because even in his unconverted state, he had picked up on the religion-threatening whiff of freedom that surrounded the earliest believers in Jesus as Lord and Messiah. So he goes to Damascus, with letters patent from the managers of his religion, to round up the offenders and bring them bound to Jerusalem for trial.

But on the way, Jesus appears to him — or so we assume, if we don't pay attention to the text. Although Paul later on says he *saw* the risen Lord (1 Cor. 15:9), this passage in Acts belies that. When he gets near Damascus, what he *sees* is a blinding light flashing around him (περιήστραψεν, v. 3). The parallels (and also the differences) between Saul in Acts 9 and the blind man in John 9 are startling. Not only doesn't Saul lay eyes on Jesus; when Jesus does speak to him after he falls on the ground ("Saul, Saul, why are you persecuting *me*?"), the question has got to seem as weird to him as "Do you believe in the Son of Man?" did to the blind beggar. He's persecuting *heretics*, for heaven's sake, not God. He's doing godly, religious work. He *knows* he's right. And like the blind man (but without his faith at this point), Saul asks nearly the same question — "Who are you, *Sir?* [κύριε]" — and he gets almost the same answer: "It's me [ἐγώ εἰμι], Jesus, whom you're persecuting." Furthermore, he gets the same kind of strange, insignificant direction about what to do: not to wash in a pool, but to go on into Damascus and wait to be told something unspecified. No miracle, no explanation; just get up, go, and do something *inconsequential*.

To his credit, Saul makes his first act of faith: he goes. It's an act that doesn't look like faith or feel like faith. But it's enough. It's faith like a grain of mustard seed, and it's all the risen Lord needs. It gets Saul up off the ground, and it gets him to open his eyes (a sensible move: how else would he find his way along the road to Damascus again?). But the main thing about it is that it brings him to the discovery that *he's blind*. Up until now, he's had his eyes closed to shield them from the brilliance of the light; he apparently assumes that it's safe to open them now and take a look at whom he's dealing with. Yet he sees nothing. His companions have to lead him by the hand — which, since *they* don't seem to have been blinded, proves it wasn't the light that got Saul; it was the hidden plan of Jesus himself.

Think of what Saul *doesn't* know at this juncture. He can't be sure his blindness isn't a punishment for hounding Jesus; but he probably has a number of minds on that subject: "Jesus is dead; how can I fairly be said to be persecuting him?" "Why should I be struck blind for doing my religious duty as I see it?" "What in the Name of God is going on here?" "What am I supposed to do in Damascus while I wait; see an ophthalmologist?" Moreover, there are other things he doesn't know at all. He doesn't know he's being called by Jesus to be an apostle, or to become the principal architect of the doctrine of grace, or to end up as the great-granddaddy of Christian theology. He doesn't know that his blindness is going to be only a three-day special: for all he knows, he'll be blind for the rest of his life. He doesn't know beans about the "believer," Ananias, whom Jesus is going to send to him when he gets to the city — except that he's got to suspect, when this Ananias shows up, that he'll punch Saul out as soundly as Pilate's soldiers did the blindfolded Jesus in the praetorium. All he knows, after spending three days blind, hungry, and thirsty ("he neither ate nor drank"; v. 9), is that he's got nothing left: he's an *empty vessel*.

Do you see what that says to us as preachers? It says that all Jesus needs is our emptiness. It says that unless we're willing to be blind to the certainties of religion by which we've lived our lives, we'll never be able to hear the Word of God, let alone preach it. For the blind depend on hearing to a degree that the seeing never come close to. We're not called to *read* the Scriptures — not to search them with our eyes or get them down pat by our knowledge, and certainly not to see them through the lenses of a correct religious understanding. We're called to come to them blind to everything religion ever told us we were supposed to expect, and just *hear them*. Because while seeing may be an analogy to knowledge, *hearing* is the classic analogue of *faith*. And faith is always *trust* in a person's *word*. It's not a tissue of understandings or doctrines. It's not assent to religious propositions. It's a blind trust in Someone who calls us into emptiness so that then — *in* that emptiness, not after we've gotten bravely over it — we can hear *him*.

Our dealings with Scripture are not to be learned studies, or the drawing of pious conclusions, or the discovery of lessons that will lead us into spiritual growth. They're to be blind searches in which we have nothing to guide us but "the drawing of this Love and the Voice of this calling" (T. S. Eliot, *Little Gidding*). Good preachers come to the Bible as Saul came into Damascus: with their eyes and mouths shut and their ears and hearts open. They don't try to hear the odd snatches of cult, creed, and conduct they can arm-wrestle out of Scripture — not the tough stuff of religion and moralism, but the Good News about which God wants the world to trust him. Moreover, since the blind alone understand the importance of that kind of listening, no preachers will hear Jesus until they refuse to see anything else. "I determined not to know anything among you, save Jesus Christ, and him crucified"

(1 Cor. 2:2; KJV). "I once was lost, but now am found,/was blind, but *now* I see."

The best preachers work in the dark. They never try to get their old religious vision back; they learn to walk through Scripture by listening — and by being empty enough to let the Word they hear speak through them.

*   *   *

So much, then — or so little — for *faith*, and not for religion or learning or talent as the preacher's exclusive guide. But I do owe you one other bit of elucidation. I've used the phrase *the Mystery of Christ* many times; and I've said that it's a mystery that lies at the roots of the being of every creature, bar none. Nevertheless, since that may have seemed like a fast shuffle to you, I want to try and say it at slightly greater length. (Yes, I know: I'm circling back to mere knowledge again, and if you've taken in what I've said about faith, you feel you have the right to call me on it. You do. But I never said that getting over our passion for knowing was easy, or even likely. Besides, in my defense, this isn't a sermon. Your irritation is the price you pay for getting yourself involved in a conversation with a theologian.)

In one of my earlier books (*The Parables of Judgment*), I illustrated the presence of the Mystery of Christ — of the Word of God incarnate throughout all of time and space — by likening it to an iceberg floating beneath the surface of history. Since icebergs float nine-tenths down and one-tenth up, that gave me the idea of saying that the incarnation of God in Christ worked the same way. If you go down *below* history at any moment whatsoever, you find the one, single iceberg of the *Word made flesh* lying right beneath your feet: that's the *hidden* presence of the Mystery of Christ. But if you look across the *surface* of history, you see portions of that same iceberg sticking up in plain sight — you see *upthrustings* of Jesus the Word into the events of history: those are the *revealed* presences of the Mystery.

As it turns out, that illustration worked nicely. For one thing, it let me see Abel's murder as one of the earliest revelations of the death of Christ, which is the key to history. For another, it took all those barren women in Genesis and made them the incarnate Wisdom of God disclosing her penchant for making emptiness the principal device of salvation. For a third, it made the Paschal Lamb in Exodus the incarnate Word himself, not a mere analogy to him. And for one more, it enabled me to take seriously Paul's insistence that the Rock in the wilderness was not just a metaphor for Christ but *Jesus in Person*.

Now, however, I want to *play* with that notion. I want to melt the iceberg and talk about water instead of ice. In addition to providing me with a warmer illustration of the Mystery of Christ, it will have the added advantage of putting one of the major images of Scripture into our chat. Watch.

Water appears all through the Bible: it's practically one of God's favorite plotting devices. At the very beginning of Genesis (after God establishes the basic distinction between the heavens and the earth), the first thing he arranges to have lying around in creation is the *waters* upon which the Spirit of God moved. In addition, in the second creation story (in chapter two — in the "dry" as opposed to the "wet" account of creation), there is a *stream* that rises from the earth and waters the whole face of the ground. And the imagery goes on and on. There are the waters of the Red Sea and of the cloud by day in which the Israelites were baptized. There is (to say it again) the water they drank from the Rock in the desert. There are the waters of the Jordan that stood up to let them cross over into the Promised Land. There are those same waters in Jesus' baptism. There is Jesus himself as living water. There is the water and the blood from his side in death. And for good measure, when the Scriptures come to their happy ending in the book of Revelation, the river of Eden returns as the River of Life, bright as crystal, flowing out of the throne of God and of the Lamb in the New Jerusalem. Not bad for mere H_2O.

But now consider how water reveals the Mystery of Christ in

the *ordinary exchanges of life in the world.* All life comes from the sea; and once that life graduates to dry land (no insult intended to the fishes), it continues to live from the sea. The waters of the oceans evaporate and form cloud cover; the clouds turn into rain and snow; the melt goes into the ground; the runoff goes into the rivers; and the rivers flow back into the sea to start the cycle all over again. The water is never *not* there — and the Mystery of Christ, in both creation and redemption, is never not there, either.

Now then: think of the Mystery of Christ as water, and play with it. In one sense, the presence of the incarnate Word in human nature is like *standing* water — like the water in an aquifer. It's the water table from which every living thing draws the water of life — the vegetation drawing it from the ground, and the animals drawing it from the plants and other animals. (This last, perhaps, represents the *dark side* of the exchanges of the Mystery, the way in which the life of Christ fills us in death — in the laying down of life by friend for friend.) But where the ground lies low enough, the water table emerges as lakes and ponds where the water is *manifest.* (These, possibly, are the saints who lie low enough in the world to let the Mystery that fills them be revealed.) And in the great troughs of the earth, where the ground lies lowest of all, the standing water appears as the oceans teeming with life.

You'll have to pardon me: I can't resist whimsy here. Why shouldn't I make Jesus the Pacific, since he's the largest manifestation of the Living Water that stands beneath the surface of history? Why shouldn't I make the church catholic the Atlantic, since it now manages to cover both hemispheres? Why shouldn't I make your congregation the Antarctic, since the Mystery stands beneath it, too, covered though it may be with a religious ice-pack? Why indeed shouldn't I make you as their preacher the smallest ocean of all, the Arctic, since under whatever frozenness may clothe you, the Living Water, and him crucified, still lies?

On the other hand, the presence of the Mystery of Christ in the world is like water under pressure — like the water of an *artesian* well. It's the *living* water of the creating, redeeming Word who bursts upward into history and showers it with the manifest power of his incarnation — with the "mighty acts" by which the Mystery reveals itself. So to continue the whimsy in a more serious vein, might we not say that the Creation, the Passover, the Prophets, the Cross, and the Resurrection are precisely such manifestations? That wouldn't be a bad tack to take; but the distinction between standing water and artesian water needs still more attention, because Jesus himself used it in his conversation with the Samaritan woman in the fourth chapter of John. Consider the scene.

The lady has come to draw water out of a well. (John anticipates his story's punch line here by calling it a πηγή, a "spring," a "fountain"; but he's getting ahead of himself.) Jesus, sitting by the well because he's tired, asks her for a drink. She doesn't give him one, though: instead, she gives him a little smart-mouthed chitchat about Jewish-Samaritan relations. To which Jesus replies, *"If you knew the gift of God, and who it is who's saying to you, 'Give me a drink,' you would have asked him, and he would have given you living water* [ὕδωρ ζῶν]*."* To which she replies with another of her flip remarks: *"Sir* [κύριε, "mister"], *you haven't got a bucket, and the well is deep"* [she uses the word φρέαρ for the well: it means a "hole," a "pit," a "shaft"]; *"where are you going to get this living water from?"* (All she means at this moment is *"Where's this spring water you're talking about as opposed to the plain old well-water we're stuck with here?"*)

In response, Jesus works a flip of his own on her. Not missing a beat, he picks up on her use of φρέαρ and makes a revelation out of correcting her usage. He tells her, *"Everyone who drinks of this water will thirst again; but whoever drinks of the water that I will give him will never thirst as long as the ages last; and the water that I will give him will become in him a* πηγή [spring] *of water* ἁλλομένου [leaping up] *to eternal life."* But the woman, still at no loss for words, doesn't miss a beat, either. Her answer to him is a triumph of conceding her opponent's case while not letting him think she's impressed. She begins by addressing Jesus with the same word as before (the word is κύριε again; but this time the author of the Gospel intends us to read it as *Lord* and to hear it as a pun intended by the woman —

as a wry act of faith, if you will): *"Lord,"* she says, *"give me this water so I'll never be thirsty or have to keep schlepping here with a bucket all the time."* But the clincher is that for the rest of the story, the woman never bothers to get herself any water! She leaves her water-pot at the well and goes into the city to tell people about Jesus. The whole point of the passage (and I apologize for my slowness in getting to it) is that even for foot-dragging characters like the Samaritan woman, or you, or me, faith in Jesus the Living Water is all we need. Once again, therefore, *Q.E.D.*

But enough of these excursions through Scripture for now. I've made them partly as an example of what you might do by *listening* to what Scripture says rather than by coming to it with eyes fastened on cult, creed, and conduct. But mostly, I've made them in the hope of moving you, if possible, into the *freedom* — into the *larking around* you'll enjoy if you preach out of nothing but the grace of the cross. I want to move you into the liberty of blind faith in the Living Water himself who bursts like a fountain into your emptiness.

Not that you have to be perfectly blind or utterly empty. You and I have depended on our sight and our knowing for far too long to expect that we'll arrive quickly (or ever) at such a state. The way we are, it's tough enough to catch even a glimpse of the Mystery. As a comedian once said, "It's hard to explain bad taste to people who actually have it." It's even harder to persuade preachers who've tried all their lives to be *something* that they need only to be *nothing* — and to trust Jesus to do the rest. But that, as the man said, is what it's all about: "To me, to live is Christ, and to die is gain" (Phil. 1:21). I wish you luck. I hope you get thirsty enough, and dried up enough, and withered enough, and shriveled away to nothing enough to come at least within hailing distance of being nobody at all. Because until you're that, you'll never amount to anything as a preacher.

It's now time for me to stop being a menace and try to give you practical help. If you're a preacher, I have a few more tricks up my sleeve that will stand you in good stead — though I can't promise I'll stifle my criticisms completely. If you're a member of a congregation, I hope you'll just hang in here with me. As I said at the outset, you're as much a part of the Gospel-proclaiming enterprise as your pastor is. Knowing what he or she is up against might even make you a more understanding friend.

PART TWO

THE PRACTICE
OF PREACHING

SEVEN

The Ingredients of Preaching

In the second half of this book, I'm going to give you a guided tour through the practicalities of producing a sermon — or, more modestly put, a short trip through the inside of my head to show you my views on the subject. But before I do, I want to prepare you by setting down a few home truths about preachers and preaching.

The first can be put briefly. Great sermons will always be in short supply. Even in the case of first-rate preachers, the church occasionally has to settle for third-rate performances. And in the case of second-rate preachers . . . well, let's just say that there are more of them than any other kind. That's not a criticism. It's one of the facts of church life. I'd only make matters worse if I tried to change the situation by making preachers feel guilty about it. It's that way in every occupation. The world's supply of top-notch saxophonists is minuscule compared with the armies of honkers who live down the street from you — and the same thing goes for plumbers, professors, and for you as a preacher. Rating you (or worse yet, giving you the impression that I have a secret formula for lifting you from second-rate status to first, or even from tenth to fifth) is not what I'm up to here.

Sure, you would love to take home an Oscar for your performance in the pulpit; but for most of us, that's never going to happen. And sure, if you're a lay person, you probably think your church has a God-given right to a pastor who can do drama, tragedy, and shtick right up there with the best of them — and do it all every Sunday in fifteen minutes or less. But neither of you is likely to get such a prize. What you'll have to settle for is the preacher you already are, or the one you already have. "What's good is difficult, and what's difficult is rare": paragons will always be rare birds. So ratings — and all the heavy breathing, heartache, and log-rolling that go into the giving and getting of them — are irrelevant to the subject of preaching.

The trouble with them is that they're based on the wrong comparison. Instead of applying a germane category to what preachers are supposed to do, they slap the restaurant-critic's "star" system on them. "★" or "★★" for the relatively decent performers, "★★★★" for the spellbinders — and the ignominious "no stars" for the rest of us. The comparison is worse than wrong; it's mischievous. It tempts congregations into the grandiose notion that they're hiring homiletical chefs to serve them four-star food, when what they should be doing is marrying themselves to someone who, with a little help and a bushel of luck, may turn out to be a decent *household cook*.

To use a word that's momentarily out of fashion, parish preachers are supposed to be *housewives*. Their principal job is to serve their family nourishing and flavorful meals. That's an illustration I can accept. It gives us all the nice, low expectation that what they feed us will be conducive to health, not Christian dyspepsia. If God can manage to keep the human race alive and well with the assortment of average-to-worse home cooks he puts up with, he can certainly do the same for the church. Or, to change the illustration slightly, preachers should think of themselves as the *mothers* of their parishes — or the fathers, not to neglect the male cooks among us, in or out of the pulpit. (I admit that putting the clergy *in loco parentis* like that has its dangers: it can easily tempt them into acting like know-it-alls and disciplinarians. Still, those titles don't necessarily suggest ruling high-handedly over a rabble of offspring; primarily, they suggest a *nurturing* role: a role that involves feeding the mother and/or father as well as the children.)

56

Accordingly, I want you to think about the preacher as cook and feeder — or possibly even as a mere slicer, dicer, pot-stirrer, and dish-washer. One of my many odd callings has been to be a food writer who also happens to do most of the shopping, prepping, cooking, and garbage-hauling in my own home. So I do have some expertise in dealing with the illustration I'm urging on you. As a household cook, for example, I'm an apostate from the religions of food and diet that now plague this once-great nation. (I'm not talking about fast food: I happen to think Big Macs and Egg McMuffins are fine.) What bothers me is the late-twentieth-century's penchant for doctrinaire pronouncements on the subject of cooking and eating. For example: It's gotten so bad that when people are watching me at the stove — when I've turned off the heat and start to stir four tablespoons of cold butter (yes, I said *butter!*) into my *Bolognese* sauce to round out the flavor and take up the floating grease (yes, that *works!*) — I have to chase the true believers out of the kitchen lest their pious consciences be offended. Such people don't cook or dine; they sniff around for heresies — and have fits when they find them. Does that sound like the trouble religion gives preachers in their congregations, or what?

Moreover, as a working writer on food, I have the same problems. There's a bushel of bad theology covering up the real subject in the kitchen as well as in the church. The temple police of the food establishment (food-page editors) are just as dreadful as the religion-and-morals cops among the faithful. They berate us with creed, cult, and conduct until almost everything written about food turns into a commandment. "Thou shalt not eat sodium, cholesterol, or calories." "Thou shalt diet, consume fluids, and use polyunsaturated oils."

Notice, if you will, the madness of such prescriptions. They're all abstractions and generalities — and they're jargon to boot. No prudent person would try to put sodium on her food; she'd ask you to pass the salt. No sane person would ever request a fluid; he'd ask for wine, beer, water, or a Coke. And for the first three thousand millennia of our evolution, it never occurred to persons of any kind that there were such nonentities as calories. Calories aren't things, for earth's sake; they're only *measurements*. It wasn't until a fraction of a second ago in the long day of human history that we came to believe such creatures of air and darkness existed and had the power to do us mischief. Up till then, we just knew that too much grease would tend to make us gross and that fasting till we fainted would make us thin — and we let it go at that. In short, we occupied ourselves with facts, not pharisaism. In our cooking, we had our wits about us, not a religion that took all the fun out of it.

In our history as the church, that same preference for religion over reality, for the consolations of doctrine over the taste of grace, has occupied us even more — almost from our very beginning. It wasn't long after his ascension that Jesus had to get Saul to rescue him from the commandment factory the church was trying to remodel the kitchen of grace into. But the pharisees of religion are no better than the pharisees of food. As the diet mongers revise their edicts from on high every month (olive oil used to be out; now it's in), so the commandment mavens in the church re-chisel their tables of stone every decade. Especially lately. In the sixties, you could go all huggy-kissy, even in church; now you can't. Since the seventies, ethnic jokes have been a no-no. It makes you long for a time when we'll be able to get back to where Augustine, on one of his better days, tried to put us: *"Ama, et fac quod vis,"* he said — Love first; then go do anything you please.

I shall not belabor that subject further. It's time now to set the preacher-as-household-cook illustration on the counter and have a look at what's supposed to go into the dish we're getting ready to cook. Because it's the ingredients of a dish that good cooks and good preachers most delight in. They revel in the *fascinating strangeness* of the stuff they've got to work with. A real cook, for example, will *regale* you with his or her delight at the way flour and fat combine to thicken a sauce. A good preacher will speak *enchantingly* of the startling seasonings that Jesus pokes into his parables — or be *astonished* at the lardoons of craftiness and criminality with which the Lord laces his life.

Augustine did that on occasion. *"Crux muscipulum diaboli,"* he once said in a sermon: "The cross is a mousetrap for the devil." Then he proceeded to wax whimsical about the devil spotting the bait of God's death in the trap, and he had him smack his lips at the thought of getting his teeth into it — only to discover that, in the resurrection, the bait turned out to be fake.

John Donne did much the same kind of thing in his famous Christmas sermon:

> In paradise, the fruits were ripe, the first minute, and in heaven it is alwaies Autumne, his mercies are ever in their maturity. We ask *panem quotidianam,* our daily bread, and God never sayes you should have come yesterday, he never sayes you must againe to morrow, but *to day if you will heare his voice,* to day he will heare you. . . . Though in the wayes of fortune, or understanding, or conscience, thou have been benighted till now, wintred and frozen, clouded and eclypsed, damped and benummbed, smothered and stupefied till now, now God comes to thee, not as in the dawning of the day, not as in the bud of spring, but as the Sun at noon to illustrate all shadowes, as the sheaves in harvest, to fill all penuries, all occasions invite his mercies, and all times are his seasons.

Admittedly, those two are a hard act to follow, but I'll try. Because in one less-than-fell swoop, they bring me to the most important ingredient of preaching with which the preacher must play: *the Scriptures.* There is no substitute (and certainly no doctrinal or ethical substitute) for the preacher's playful astonishment at the strange comestibles with which the Scriptures are filled — for the *fun* he or she must have with the Bible's artichokes and asparagus. Jesus, for example, puts the most bizarre items into his discourses: *mayhem and murder* into a parable of grace (The King's Son's Wedding); *faith* into a parable about a businessman away on a trip (The Talents); *snotty characters* as exemplars of faith (The Ten Virgins); and *nefarious behavior* as a virtue (The Treasure Hidden in a Field;

The Unjust Steward). And in his *acted parables* (that is, in the salient events of his life, such as his breaking of the Sabbath or his shameful death on the cross), he holds up *criminality* as the very thing God uses to make the stew of history come out right. So it simply won't do for a preacher to come at those peculiarities with the doctrinal mind-set of a dieter. You have to taste their odd flavors, not analyze them or put an intellectual straitjacket on them. You're a cook, for God's sake, not a critic.

How then do you go about that tasting? Well, like a cook, you have to spend a lot of time dipping your finger into the sauce of Scripture just because you like to dip. There's nothing worse than preachers who come to a Bible passage thinking they have to get something out of it, or worse yet, trying to work into it some concoction they've had in the freezer for years. The only way they can become decent preachers is to be willing to taste everything in the Scriptures with a clean palate. Once they start down the road of deciding whether they approve of something, or can make a popular use of it, they're doomed — right along with the congregations they serve — to a diet of nothing but leftovers.

I know. I said I would put the comparison down, and I shall — as soon as this paragraph is over. I have to give it one more playful poke. I could give you the bromidic advice that you should read the Bible *a lot,* but you've probably heard that suggestion so often (and maybe done so little about it) that it's useless for me to put it that way. Instead, I'm going back into the kitchen — where I'll give you better advice: make Scripture the *pantry* of your preaching. In particular, learn how to appreciate the unique flavors of its bounty of calf's feet, Calvados, and tripe. Sniff at its basil, marjoram, rosemary, and thyme until you discover how to use them as the *spice* of your homiletical cooking.

There! I think I've gotten the illustration out of my system. Here goes plain advice.

My first suggestion to you is not that you read the Bible regularly. *Regularly* is a word that's been so often applied to Scripture that it makes the Bible sound like little more than a remedy for homiletical constipation. But even if that's not your problem, you're too busy being a pastor who has to show up at committee meetings, lawn fairs, and clean-up days — and who must deal with parishioners who elevate paper cuts into Parkinson's disease — to have free time even for ordinary regularity.

Nor am I going to urge you to read the Bible at all. *Reading* Scripture (at least as we commonly read other printed matter) is just as idle a suggestion. The trick is to *hear* the Scriptures, not simply look at them, or make a study of them, or turn them into proof texts for your pet theological system. The Lord has indeed made Scripture *God's Word Written* (by using the Holy Spirit's body-English — or body-Hebrew, or body-Greek); but you mustn't stick at the *words* of Scripture to the detriment of the Word himself. In the Bible, "the Word of the Lord" is always *Someone speaking to you*, not just someone writing memos for you to read at your desk. Indeed, if you glance at the history of reading, you'll find that perusing words silently was a late development: for millennia, people always read *aloud* (or else they moved their lips to *hear* the words in their minds). The first recorded instance of our now confirmed habit of reading to ourselves (and lately, of thinking that moving our lips is a sin, or that skimming is a skill worth acquiring) occurred when Augustine observed Anselm of Milan *not* moving his lips when he read. Our reading to ourselves has brought us to the sorry state where the only place adults are read to out loud anymore is in church.

I don't mean to carp. I want only to make a couple of suggestions about *hearing* the Scriptures. First, don't wait until you have free, quiet time for listening to them; make yourself some "slave" time instead. Tell those imperious chairpersons that you can't attend their meetings at eight in the morning because the Boss won't let you. This may come as a surprise, since they're under the impression that you work for them, not God; but don't even think of showing up. And tell all those parishioners with problems that can't wait till you get to the office that, unfortunately, you can't talk to them right now because . . . well, you make it up. Tell them you're in the middle of a session with your own Counselor. Tell them you have a migraine. Tell them your house is on fire. Tell them your husband has just told you he's sick of living with a pastor and wants a divorce. Tell them anything; and then tell them you'll see them at one.

Second, when you do sequester time to be free enough to listen to the Scriptures, do it by reading the *Daily Office*. If the ecclesiastical outfit you belong to doesn't provide you with the texts and lesson calendars for that exercise, steal a prayer book from somebody else's outfit. Then read the Office *every single day,* Sundays included. God may take Saturdays off, but don't you even think about skipping the Lord's Day. You're not too busy then, either: you can always get up earlier and attend to it in the last half hour you would have spent asleep.

Next, when you read the Office, read it *out loud*. You're supposed to be *hearing* the Word of God, not looking it over. If it embarrasses you to be heard muttering in your study, embarrass yourself even more and go into the church proper and declaim it at the top of your voice. You'll soon get over your heebie-jeebies.

Next, when you read the lessons in the Office, never think of yourself as "studying the Bible." That's for Scripture scholars, not preachers. You're supposed to be *falling in love* with the Word — with the Beloved in whom you're accepted — not proving that your interest in Scripture is intellectually respectable. Even Scripture scholars (when and if they're good preachers) rarely strike that smarmy, self-congratulatory note. They always seem more smitten than smart — more like lovers than pedants.

Last of all, read the Office till you die. Slog through its two-year cycle of readings for as many years as the Lord leaves you in this vale of pointless busyness. You're not reading it because you like what you see but because the church has told you to listen to what you hear. In the old days, Roman priests used to refer to their Breviary (which admittedly was rather stingy when it came to Bible lessons) as their "wife." Your Office is simply your "old lady." Stay with her long enough, and you'll come to appreciate even her tirades, her boring conversations, and her faults.

I do have to add one thing. Reading the Office is no substitute for wrestling with Scripture until it pins your shoulders to the mat. The most available time you have for that exercise is when you prepare your sermons — and the best resource you have for it is the *Eucharistic* Lectionary for the Sundays and Holy Days of the Church Year. First of all, *use* the Lectionary. Don't give me that old line about wanting to choose your own lessons because it will help you speak from your heart. You must not use your so-called heart — or any of your other devices and desires — to cook up some topical marvel of a sermon. Topical sermons are like topical anesthetics: they don't go deep.

Accordingly, when you do come to sit yourself down with the readings for a given Sunday, don't skim through them and say things like, "Ah! The good old Prodigal Son: I guess it'll have to be Repentance all over again." Or, "What on earth am I supposed to say about the Lord's Prayer and The Friend at Midnight this time around?" Instead, read the passage over and over out loud. *Listen* to it until you stop trying to fit it into what you've already figured out. *Open your ears* to the things you've never noticed before. Like the fact that the parable of The Prodigal Son is misnamed: its proper name should be *The Forgiving Father.* Or like the fact that there are three deaths in that parable. The *father* dies at the very beginning when he drops dead legally by putting his will into effect while he's still alive. The *prodigal,* though, has a harder time of it. You hear a distinction: he's only half-dead when he first formulates his confession at the hog trough in the far country; he isn't thoroughly dead until, in his father's arms, he stops trying to con his way into being a hired hand and admits he has no existence at all as a son. And the *fatted calf* ends up just plain dead. He enters the scene, in fact, as the Christ figure — as the festive roast that makes the homecoming a real bash, and not just fried rice and egg rolls from the Chinese take-out.

You can do the same kind of thing with The Friend at Midnight, if you listen to it *playfully* enough. But you'll have to break your dependency on the English versions — either by reading the story in Greek (if you can), or (if you can't) at least by having a go at the Greek words to hear if they ring any bells in your head. If you're in the second boat, having a good Scripture program in your computer is a help. (For what it's worth to you, I'm currently using *Bible Works* from *Hermeneutika* in Windows 3.1, with Microsoft Word 6.0 as my writing engine: it's terrific, and practically bugless.) What a good Bible program enables you to do, among other things, is to run the English versions you're consulting parallel to the Greek: that way you can see the original Greek word, even if a particular version may have used two or three different English words to translate it. Then you can search the rest of the New Testament (if that's where your reading comes from) for all the other uses of that word to see if they ring more bells. And then . . . well, maybe you'll even come up with a sermon that's closer to the Word of God than your usual efforts.

By the way. Don't tell me you haven't got a computer or a Scripture program. You can do the same thing with an interlinear New Testament, a couple of versions, and Young's Concordance. The Index-Lexicons in the back of Young's will give you all the KJV translations of any given Hebrew or Greek word. Then, in the analytical concordance that makes up most of the book, you can look up each and every passage in which those English words occur. You can, in short, get down to listening to the original word and hear the shading of its meanings, and the puns on it in Hebrew and Greek that were in the back of the author's mind. Best of all, though, by working with the concordances of the original, you'll be building your own mental concordance in the process. Of course you won't have much room on your desk as you do all this listening. But when you're finished, there'll be a lot more room in you for the Word.

Back to The Friend at Midnight (Luke 11:5-13) as a sample of what can happen.

Verse 5: *Midnight* — (μεσονυκτίου), which contains νῦξ, which is *night* — which is when Jesus went from the Garden of Gethsemane down into the darkness of death — which is where we

64

all meet him. The *friend* who comes at that hour is φίλε, which is also the word for the *Friend* who lives in the pitch-dark house. Accordingly, the Friend inside (since this entire passage, from 11:1 to 11:13, is about prayer) is obviously either Jesus or God — or both at once, if you have any decent theology about the incarnation of God the Son in Jesus, and about the coinherence of the Persons of the Trinity.

Now then. When the friend outside shows up, the One inside refuses to give him the bread he's asking for. Radical peculiarity here: God, apparently, has a thing for saying no before he says yes. But it isn't so peculiar after all: he reveals the law before he reveals grace; he meets Nicodemus at night and gives him riddles, not understanding — and he refuses the world's endless requests for signs and gives it the darkness of the whale's belly and of the sealed tomb.

Verse 7: The Friend answers, *"Don't bother me* [μή μοι κόπους πάρεχε]; *the door* [θύρα] *is already shut, and my little children* [παιδία] *are with me in bed* [εἰς τὴν κοίτην]; *I cannot rise* [ἀναστὰς] *to give you anything."* Doesn't that put the God who's supposed to answer our prayers down in the dark all over again? Isn't it just possible that the parable is telling you he chooses first of all to be in death, and not to respond to any of the requests by which we try to get a life? Might it not be about the death and resurrection of God in Christ, which are so unsatisfying and mystifying to our managerial minds? Might it not be about his death in our own death? Keep those questions in your ear and move on.

Verse 8: *"I tell you,"* Jesus says of the Friend, *"even though he won't rise again* [ἀναστὰς] *and give him anything because the man is his friend, still, because of his shameless persistence* [διά γε τὴν ἀναίδειαν αὐτοῦ], *he will, having risen* [or being risen: ἐγερθεὶς], *give him as much as he needs."*

And that hardly scratches the surface of the passage. You've only touched on the "resurrection language" of ἀναστὰς and ἐγερθεὶς. You haven't done a thing with the deliberately brief prayer (vv. 1-4) that Jesus gives the disciples when they ask him to teach them to pray like John the Baptist's disciples. You haven't done nearly enough with the word "friend" (φίλον; search on .φιλ* and see what you come up with) — and you've done nothing yet with verses 9 to 13, in which Jesus says that God will grant any request that happens to pop out of your childish mouth. So you wrestle with that contradiction — until you get to the end, when he says, *"If you then, being evil, know how to give good gifts to your children, how much more will the Father* [πατήρ, which takes you back to the first word of the Lord's Prayer — and which some say can be read as "Daddy"] *give the Holy Spirit to those who ask him?"*

So you think for a minute, and you notice that Jesus doesn't say "to those who ask him specifically for the Holy Spirit" but simply "to those who ask him" — presumably, for anything whatsoever. (It's like the old joke about the high colonic at the Waldorf-Astoria: no matter how much you want something else, you get the spinach soup one way or another.) But then you remember that Jesus also said somewhere that the Holy Spirit, the Comforter (παράκλητος), when he comes, will lead them into all truth. So you search on .comfort*, or .παρακλητ*, and you end up in John 16, where besides saying that the Comforter will lead them into all truth, Jesus adds that the Holy Spirit *"will not speak of himself but will speak only what he hears, and will tell you* [ἀναγγελεῖ, meaning "announce," "proclaim"] *the things that are coming. He will glorify me, because he will take of what is mine and proclaim it* [ἀναγγελεῖ] *to you."*

In the end, that takes you straight back to all the "my," "me," and "I" on the lips of the Friend inside who doesn't give you what you want when you want it. He gives you what *he* has in mind — and not until after he's been dead asleep in bed and risen up. And that takes you to Jesus in his death and resurrection. And you're back on track again. And by George, you've almost got a sermon on your hands.

Just one comment. It's not always easy to do that kind of listening — and there are times in the church year when the Eucharistic Lectionary makes it positively difficult. There are flat spots on the liturgical-reading wheel. In Year C, for example, you'll spend

66

a month of Sundays after Pentecost trying to cope with Gospels from Luke 11, 12, and 13. Perhaps you'll even make a note to sit out those Sundays on vacation next year and come back when you can deal with Luke 14, where Jesus is at supper in the Pharisee's house and gives the parable of The Great Banquet. But don't. That dead stretch is worth whatever while you put into it. It's all *the Word* who speaks you out of death into life.

*   *   *

There's only one other ingredient of your preaching that I would put in the same category as Scripture, and that's *prayer*. Once again, I'm not going to give you the usual advice. I won't tell you to pray regularly, or like mad, or till your knees ache. Better yet, I shall refrain from giving you the shopworn advice to "develop your spiritual life." That's partly because I have about as much native spirituality as a rutabaga. My entire prayer life has consisted of three things: reading the Office daily (sometimes publicly in church, but more often alone in my study or car); celebrating the Eucharist daily (in church every morning for the first twenty-seven years of my priesthood, and at home with my wife Valerie for the last twenty); and saying, as often as I can remember to, a form of the Jesus prayer to the rhythm of my breathing:

> *Jesus, Jesus, Jesus;*
> *Jesus, Jesus, Jesus;*
> *Jesus, Jesus, Jesus, Jesus;*
> *I love you, I love you, I love you.*

That's *it*. I have no further expertise with which to guide you into prayer. I do, however, have a few things to say about it that may guide you away from certain attitudes I think are off the mark.

For one thing, using the phrase "the spiritual life" when talking about prayer has always struck me as a dangerous piece of puffery. Urging such a noble-sounding enterprise on people gives them the impression that there's a finer, less corporeal level they have to reach if they're to pray correctly — or to be Christians at all. That's dead wrong. God saves us in our broken-down flesh, and he raises us up with glorious bodies; he has no intention of turning us into angels or any other species of spiritual giant. Yes, we have spiritual faculties. And yes, we're allowed to sharpen them. But our honing of them is neither more nor less legitimate than our efforts at improving our psychic abilities, our business skills, our cooking performances, or our golf swing. All such activities are proper human pursuits; but none of them, not even "spirituality," is necessary for salvation — which, alas, is the air many of us seem to give off when we get all wound up about the wonderfulness of our own spiritual life (or, in particular, about the lack of such in others). Spirituality may be nice, but God doesn't depend on it to get his work done.

For another thing, prayer is not "going to God" (he's already in you), or "seeking God" (he's already found you), or "opening yourself to God" (you couldn't keep him out if you tried), or "becoming spiritual" (he's already sent you the Spirit — who would rather show you Jesus than help you display your spiritual prowess). And it's certainly not buttering God up with abject apologies for your existence — because in his Beloved Son, he already thinks you're dandy. *Prayer is just talking with Someone who's already talking to you.*

It's no fancier a subject than talking with your wife, or your husband, or the guy on the next bar stool. It's a conversation between friends, for mercy's sake, not an arcane skill you have to master. All you have to do is get free enough of your manipulative, buck-making designs on God to tell him anything that's on your mind. He's your Daddy — and he's a lot easier to talk to than any other Daddy you've run into. You can tell him you'd like a new kitchen. You can tell him you'd appreciate it if your kids stopped smoking pot. You can tell him you'd be overjoyed if your biopsy came back negative. You can tell him you'd like to stop chasing skirts . . . but not yet. You can tell him you wish you were dead. You can even be as specific as all get-out and tell him you'd love to have an eight-cylinder, 5.0 litre spiritual life with auto. trans., a/c, ww, airbags, & ABS. In short, there's nothing you can't tell him because it isn't your bright (or dim) ideas he wants most, it's *you*.

Did you notice what I did in that paragraph? I took all those things you would normally say you were *asking* God for (no matter how reverently) and turned them into *telling* God whatever happened to be on your mind. That's a nice, friendly approach to a friend. The approach we usually take with God would either switch off any other conversation-partner on the spot, or turn her into an enemy in five minutes.

The upshot, then, is this. You *must* pray if you're to be of any use to God as a preacher — or as anything else. But you must *not* pray in order to become a "good pray-er." Forget about your spiritual life. Raise your standards for prayer by lowering your sights. Prayer is whatever chitchat happens between you and God. Occasionally, when God feels like it, he gets out of bed and does something about what you tell him. Now and then, he may even give you the benefit of a few well-chosen words of response on his part. But if you've paid attention to the parable of The Friend at Midnight, you'll have noticed that Jesus doesn't give the Friend in the house a single *kind* word to say to the friend at the door. Still, he's always *there*, so just keep talking and listening. Since he never leaves *your* house, you'll never have to go away empty from his. Hang in *shamelessly* and you'll be fine.

Let me end this chapter on another personal note. I've had friends who've informed me that they hear words from God — actual *voices* — when they pray. Whenever I was told something like that, I'd say to myself, "That's nice. I think I'd like that. Why doesn't it happen to me?" But then my resident skeptic would butt in and say, "Maybe you don't want it. Maybe it wasn't God talking to them; maybe it was just an audible wish-fulfillment." And my hopeful self would shoot back, "Yeah, but what about Saul? God talked to *him*." And my intellect would say, "Look who thinks he's Paul the Apostle. Feh!"

The argument, at least for my ingenuous self, was a draw. Then one day it dawned on me that maybe God had already given me all the words I needed from him, and if I'd listen to *Scripture* and talk back to it any way I liked, that would be all the conversation I'd ever need to have a prayer life.

That's where I am now on the subject. My prayer life consists of the Eucharist, the Office, and chats with my Friend in the house of Scripture. If you already have a spiffier pattern of prayer going for you, good for you. But if you're one of those clergy whose praying is mostly professional (that is, done in public, for pay, one day a week) and not personal (that is, done inwardly, for nothing, every day), think about it. There are probably more of your type out there than any other. Although you never let the subject of your non-praying come up — not even inside your own head — you know what you are when it comes to prayer: you're a loser, a wreck, a mess. So congratulations! Up till now, you've been doing everything right. Don't muck it up by trying to turn yourself into a spiritual winner. Let me sell you my used car instead: it's the poor man's transportation to prayer, the spiritual life for klutzes. It gives you a prayer life without the bother of having to think you have to pay the bills on one. Besides, it wasn't driven anywhere except to God, so it never even left the garage. That's practically an offer you can't refuse.

Not that I'm pushing. I know you can't rush these things. But listen, it wouldn't hurt to put your money on a bargain like this.

EIGHT

Unfinished Business

Before we take off on the practicalities of sermon preparation, I think it's time to let you in on a few thoughts I've been keeping in the back of my mind. Here they are, in one short chapter.

To begin with, I never made it clear why I picked the parable of The Friend at Midnight as my main scriptural illustration in the last chapter. I did tell you that the passage (Luke 11:1-13) came from what I called a flat spot on the liturgical-reading wheel. What I didn't mention was that I chose it for that very reason. I wanted to see if I could give you an example of how listening carefully to an unpromising text (or to a text you think you've spotted some canned promise in) can lead you straight into the "precious and very great promises" themselves (2 Peter 1:4). I thought it worked pretty well, for a first stab, though you're free to think otherwise. But as a general rule for both of us, the toughest passages make the best preachers.

I also left you in the dark about why I chose the accounts of The Woman at the Well, The Man Born Blind, and The Raising of Lazarus (John, chapters 4, 9, and 11, respectively) earlier in this book. I didn't pick those passages because they were from an area of homiletical drought (to vary the metaphor). They're not: they're propers read in Lent, which is one of the choicest gardens in the church year. Moreover, they've been around a long time: their use dates back to the fourth century, when they were introduced as the

71

Gospels for the ancient "Scrutiny Masses" during the Lenten season.

Still, I didn't pick them because they were choice, or venerable, or because they illustrated something I already had in mind, or even because I thought they would be helpful to you. My choice, quite frankly, was an accident of the calendar. As I write these words, it's Maundy Thursday, 1996. I began the composition of this book on Ash Wednesday of this year, so everything I've set down so far has been written in Lent of Year A. Equally obviously, that set me up to be working on two things at once here: preaching on the assigned texts to my congregation every Sunday, and writing to you. And since the Lectionary calls for those three very long Gospels from John to be read on the third, fourth, and fifth Sundays in Lent, it just worked out that my sermon preparation was my writing preparation, and vice versa. The operation worked in reverse as well: I preached to you, and I wrote to my congregation. One hand washed the other.

I tell you all this in the hope that if you're leery about preaching from the Lectionary (or even if, like many preachers, you use it but sit loose to its texts when they don't grab you by the throat in the first two minutes), you'll be encouraged to get over those bad habits. "Man proposes, God disposes": all you have to be when you settle down to any text is *disposable*. With a preacher who's willing to sit dumbly at the feet of Scripture like Mary at the feet of Jesus (Luke 10:38-42), God can do great things. It doesn't matter if you haven't got a clue to begin with. Sit there and hang out with the passage that stumps you. If God has anything he wants you to say next Sunday, he'll get it said. His Word is already present in the words themselves. Let *them* speak to you, and the Word himself will speak through you.

One last thing I forgot to mention — or, to be honest, one more of my prejudices I haven't yet unloaded on you: my thoughts about the imperfections of the Common Lectionary we're supposed to have in common. After all my raving about it, you may be surprised to hear me badmouth it. Nevertheless, I'm convinced that unless you're aware of its shortcomings, it can turn out to be a rubber crutch. Yes, you should preach on the texts it gives you. But be careful not to put too much weight on the often-butchered passages it hands you as liturgical pericopes.

For one thing, it sometimes begins or ends its appointed readings by cutting them off from material that's essential to hearing them correctly. This is particularly a problem for preachers who take the shortcut of picking up a preprinted lesson insert for the Sunday bulletin and work on their sermons from that without ever cracking a Bible. That lame approach to sermon preparation leads them away from the text *in context* and makes them sweat a lot longer trying to break through to what the passage is really saying. Therefore, *Rule One* of a list that contains but one rule: Trust the Lectionary, but cut the cards. Always open yourself up by opening the Scriptures themselves. Start your preparation by searching the Bible and checking out what comes before and after the pericope you may be preaching on. Check as far *forward* as you must to get a firm grip on where the Holy Spirit (or his flunkies, authorial and editorial) seemed to be heading in the passage. Check as far *back* as you must in order to notice what they had in mind before they got to where you are. You're dealing with the work of a very talented committee here: neither the Spirit nor his agents were slouches when it came to structuring. There's a marvelous architecture to what they produced.

I'll give you an instance — a fresh one this time. I tripped over it three paragraphs back. When I wrote the words "like Mary at the feet of Jesus" and then paused to check the citation, a large light went on. Contrary to my own advice, I hadn't checked on the text that preceded Luke 11:1-13 when I tackled the Lord's Prayer and The Friend at Midnight in the last chapter. (Another light! It occurred to me this very moment that this parable is another case of misnaming: it ought to be called The Friend in the House, or maybe even The Friend Asleep — to get our attention off ourselves [as represented by the friend with the gimmes] and onto the God character [the Friend inside] whom Jesus introduces to add yet

another parable to his best-seller, *The Autobiography of God in Christ.*
That's just a throwaway for you to have fun with; now, back to my
exposition.)

The incident that immediately precedes Luke 11:1-13 (the
Lord's Prayer, the misnamed parable, and the wrap-up in which
Jesus says that no matter what you ask for, you're going to get the
Holy Spirit) is Jesus' Visit to Martha and Mary at the very end of
Luke 10. Some quick notes on that visit; nothing worked up. First:
Martha is a doer. She's as busy as a parish priest: a talker, a cook,
a serving girl, and a scullery maid, all rolled into one. She's also an
Olympic-class petitioner. She's so good at it that she doesn't even
ask Jesus for what she wants; she whines to him, spouting instructions as manipulative as the Psalmist's: "Don't you care that my
sister's left me to do all the work alone? Tell her to help me!"
(10:40). Second: Mary is a listener. She just sits in a swoon at the
feet of Jesus and takes him all in. Third: Jesus reads Martha the riot
act for her busyness and praises Mary for doing nothing: "Mary has
chosen the good part [τὴν ἀγαθὴν μερίδα], which will not be taken
away from her." Fourth and last: the whole passage segues perfectly
into the Lord's Prayer sequence — and into the rest of the pericope.
The disciples come to Jesus while he's resting (ὡς ἐπαύσατο), and
they ask him to do something for them (teach them to be spiritual
whizzes). Jesus, however, fobs them off with a short Daddy-prayer
and then gets down to brass tacks. Real prayer is not asking, he
tells them; it's waiting for God to get up from his nap in death and
come to you in yours. And when he does rise, Jesus insists, the
main thing he's interested in is giving you the Holy Spirit . . . et
cetera.

Nor does that take into account what comes right before The
Visit to Martha and Mary. When you look at *that,* by George, it's
the parable (again misnamed) of The Good Samaritan, which Jesus
tells in response to a lawyer in a hurry for advice about spiritual
perfection — and in which Jesus makes the defining Christ-figure
the man lying on the ground half-*dead* [ἡμιθανῆ]. Jesus slows the
lawyer down, you see. This one, though, I'll leave you to work out

on your own. (Dare I suggest a book of mine? I dare. Look it up in *The Parables of Grace*.)

Back to the Lectionary's faults. Besides lopping off the proper beginnings and endings of pericopes, it frequently chops hunks out of the middles — and for almost universally irrelevant reasons. On the one hand, it does so (presumably) to spare the troops the agony of having to listen to large doses of Scripture. But if "sermonettes make christianettes," lessonettes make preacherettes. On the other hand, it more probably does its chopping to spare the clergy the embarrassment of having to preach on verses that the compilers of the Lectionary found objectionable.

I don't have enough familiarity with other Churches' versions of the Common Lectionary to allow me to comment on what their particular liturgiologists have done in adapting it to their uses. However, I do have an unkind word for the Episcopalian arm of the liturgical *jihad*. There are times when I have a suspicion that they're a cross between biblical critics and New Age maiden aunts. On the one hand, their excisions are made to get rid of material the critics don't think much of; on the other, they're made in the name of political correctness. And all that, in deference to mere fads.

Genealogies, for example, are routinely eliminated, in spite of the fact that they're the Bible's favorite device for hanging on to the thread of the history of Salvation — and even though hearing them read aloud is an unforgettable experience, whether you enjoy it or not. For another example, ethical prescriptions (or proscriptions) that go against the grain of fashion are axed with gleeful but mystifying abandon.

To take but one instance: In the week of 6 Epiphany, in the Daily Office for Year One, the second lesson for Friday is listed as "1 Tim. 5:17-22 (23-25)." The three verses being kept from chaste eyes by the veil of "parens, verse numbers, end parens" contain the author's advice to Timothy to quit drinking water and to use a little wine to settle his stomach and cure his frequent infirmities, plus a snide but obscure aside about how some people's sins are so conspicuous that they precede them to judgment, while the sins of others follow them there — plus an innocuous comment that good works can't be hidden. It's not clear to me why the Standing Liturgical Commission of the Episcopal (of all things!) Church felt those remarks were unmentionable in front of a group that has more country club members per square foot than any other. Most Episcopalians drink like fish; and the ones who happen to be in AA (and follow the program) know perfectly well that they shouldn't use the Bible's enthusiasm for wine as an excuse for throwing away their hard-won sobriety. Whose chastity is being protected here? Or, better said, whose ox are the compilers protecting from being gored? As an Episcopal priest, my answer to the first query is, "Nobody's that I've run into lately." And my answer to the second is, "The ox of overprotective fussbudgets."

But it gets worse. Consider a more flagrant instance of the compulsion to cut: the Gospel for the Sixth Sunday after Epiphany in Year A. The citation for that pericope reads, "Matthew 5:21-24, 27-30, 33-37." Forget that such a list of numbers makes the Lectionary look more like an NFL playbook than a guide to the Bible. Forget even that my computer's Bible program won't let me retrieve chopped-up lessons like that. Notice instead the *jihad's* sly switch here from parentheses to commas. What their commas mean is that they're taking back their gracious permission to read straight through a cut if you choose and giving you a commandment not to read the omitted verses, period.

But even though they're tempting you to sentence Scripture to silence, you must always take a look at the forbidden sections. If you examine this particular instance, you'll discover that what they've carved out of the Sermon on the Mount at this point are verses 25 and 26 (in which Jesus talks about "agreeing with your adversary quickly" because if you don't, you won't get out of jail until you've paid "the last nickel"), and verses 31 and 32 (in which he carries on about divorce and remarriage being the same thing as adultery). They excised the former, apparently, in deference to a critic's opinion that it doesn't belong where Matthew, or Jesus, or the Holy Spirit put it; and they pruned out the latter because . . .

well, who knows? And who in his or her right mind cares? We're reading Scripture here, for God's sake (literally), not looking for opinions we can agree with. I've been married, divorced, and re-married; and on all three occasions I thought I was doing the right thing. But so what? I can't see how that entitles me to get up on my high horse and not listen to the Word of God as it stands (*wie es steht geschrieben,* as the Lutherans like to put it). I don't have to like it; I just have to hear it. Nobody made *me* the boss of the Bible — and I bridle at people who make themselves bosses because the Boss himself strikes them as too bossy.

Add to that the "politically correct" cuts the Lectionary makes, and you've got the full, ridiculous picture. In our grand campaign to deliver the female sex from the bondage of male domination, we occupy molehills and defend them as if they were the Alps. For example: we take aim at Paul and blow him off the map for saying that women should have their heads covered in church. The passage in which that now indefensible and trivial bit of free advice occurs (1 Cor. 11:2-16) is skipped over between Tuesday and Wednesday in Year A's Office-readings for the week of 4 Lent. The cut is a cowardly one — made, perhaps, in the hope that you won't notice the omission after a good night's sleep. But it's also a stupid one: what kind of victory is it for the cause of women's lib when your reading of Scripture is held hostage to literalists who can't tell an opinion from a revelation? Battlegrounds should be chosen more strategically than that.

Worse yet, we're not supposed to have our ears sullied by Paul's strictures that women should keep their mouths shut in church, or that the husband is the head of the wife, or that men who go to bed with other men will "receive the just recompense of their error" — presumably because there are some of us who think those notions passé. Again, so what? Such excisions don't erase the words as they stand; they simply deprive us of the opportunity to hear the problematical pronouncements of the Word Written — and of the fun of hassling each other with them. Put all those spoilsport excisions together, and you've got the devil's advice to Faust as the sovereign rule of reading Scripture: *Man darf das nicht vor keusche Ohren nennen, was keusche Herzen nicht entbehren können* ("Prim ears mustn't be told what prim hearts can't bear"). But where did we get the idea that the prim should be the arbiters of what gets read in church? I'll tell you where: from the liberal left, of all places. I'm a liberal, for crying out loud, and I still think that's ridiculous. So, to spite the liturgical terrorists, I read straight through all their cuts. I invite you to join me. At the very least, between the fundamentalists in your congregation who think those strictures are in the same league as the preface to John's Gospel and the liberals who think they're the work of the devil, you'll have some rousing coffee hours after church.

One last comment and we're done: The Common Lectionary is not even as common as it was cracked up to be. The reason? Because every Church's Lectionary Committee felt driven to diddle with it and leave their grubby denominational fingerprints on it. Lutherans, for example, sometimes aren't reading the same pericopes as Episcopalians or Romans — and even when we do have the same lessons, we occasionally find ourselves several Sundays apart when we read them. And so it came to pass that we sank the ship of synch we were supposed to be sailing. But . . .

But! But! But! For all its faults, the Common Lectionary remains the church's greatest single ecclesiastical, ecumenical, liturgical, and homiletical accomplishment of the last five hundred years, and I love it still — passionately. Back now (I detect a sigh of relief from you) to the business at hand.

NINE

Preaching from Notes

From here on out I'm going to focus quite narrowly on the business of sermon production, not even going near the subjects that are staples of homiletics courses. I have no expertise in such matters as style, delivery, or voice production. My preaching is idiosyncratic to the point of stylelessness: people have a hard time recognizing what I give them as sermons. About the highest compliment I ever get is, "That was an interesting talk you gave this morning, Father." My delivery has more faults than the state of California: I focus on the folks in the front pews rather than on projecting to the ones in the back because my eyes are not that good; I drop my voice with distressing frequency (without a body mike, my intimate little asides don't carry past the third row); and the timbre of my voice goes so easily from a resonant bass to a nasal, Queens-accented tenor that it provokes my wife (who's a singer) to wrath.

Nor am I going to discourse learnedly about the various types of sermons — exegetical, expository, topical, story-based, and what-have-you. My theory is that if you're good at those sorts of things, you'll do them naturally, and if you're not, you shouldn't try to imitate people who are. When and as I give you examples drawn from my own preaching (and I shall, because they're all I have), my sole purpose in showing you those specimens will be to illustrate certain aspects of sermon preparation, not to tell you what to do or how to do it.

Accordingly, except for the Epilogue, we're going to confine ourselves to two matters for the rest of this book. This chapter will concern itself with how to prepare for a sermon that will be preached from notes — that is, an extemporaneous sermon in the best sense of the word: one that's put into its final shape at the time and place of its delivery, not beforehand. In the next chapter, we'll talk about how to prepare a fully composed sermon that you'll read from the pulpit. Be patient with me. I'm aware that your congregation may have more tolerance for extempore sermons than for those which are read to them. There's a skin of reason on that preference, but their underrating of being read to is too often overrated by their pastors. In my book, reading a sermon is no crime. Provided you've produced a carefully prepared manuscript that's written in conversational English rather than in sociologese, psycho-babble, or academic jargon — and provided you read it *to* your people rather than *at* them — a preachment that's read can be every bit as happy an experience for them as any other.

A word about my qualifications for both enterprises and we're on our way. I'm in a position to tell you about preaching from notes because, as I've said, I've preached that way (with some proficiency, I think) for forty-seven years. On the other hand, while I rarely read from a prepared text, I'm still able to give you advice about writing because I'm a writer who's been paid (mostly not a lot) for twenty-four books of my own, two rewrites of other people's work, and many drawersful of food articles and dog-work journalism. That's not to brag; it's all been a gift. Don't envy me, though. For your comfort, I can tell you that I've written badly so often (and in the process, picked up a few hints about how to do it better) that I may be the very harbor-pilot you need, no matter which homiletical boat you're in.

*   *   *

By and large, I think most preachers would do better to preach from notes than from a manuscript. I say that not because it's my own custom but because I think most of them preach better that way, even if they don't realize it. I'll try to prove it to you by citing bad homiletical habits on both sides of the pulpit railing. Naturally, my experience of extempore sermons has been with Episcopalian versions of them. Still, you've probably heard (or given) them in your Church, so if you make the necessary allowances, I think you'll see what I'm getting at.

For the past twelve years, I served as the assistant priest in a large parish. We had two services every Sunday (both of them Communion) at 8:00 and 10:00 a.m. Right from the start of my time there (by the kindness of the rector), both of us preached every Sunday: if I preached the homily at the eight o'clock service on a given day, I would be the Celebrant at the ten — and vice versa in the case of the rector. The next week, we would switch roles: he would preach at eight, and I at ten — and so on through the year, with minor exceptions for vacations and absences.

Bad habit number one, therefore. People would sometimes ask me, "Are you preaching this Sunday?" — meaning, in their heart of hearts, "Are you *really* preaching this week, or are you just doing a quickie for the troops who have an early date at the first tee?" My answer to them was never anything but "Yes." I wasn't about to explain that I preach every Sunday — or that, according to the Book of Common Prayer, every Eucharist has to have a sermon — for the simple reason that I always put in the same amount of time preparing my notes whether I was giving a homily (not a sermonette) at eight or preaching what they considered a genuine sermon at ten. If they wanted to hear me badly enough, they could figure out the schedule for themselves and get up earlier every other Sunday.

Bad habit number two. Sadly, a lot of preachers make the same assumption as the laity. They think their homilies don't have to be serious sermons. If they can manage to make solemn noises for nine minutes, they consider their day's preaching done. This is more often the case with "manuscript preachers" than with "note preachers" — but it's a struggle for all of us not to go with the downhill flow. On a few occasions, when my rector was suddenly taken ill on a morning he was supposed to have the ten o'clock sermon, there would be earnest questions in the sacristy before we went into the "main" service. People would ask me (even those who heard me preach earlier at the eight), "Are you going to skip the sermon?" My answer in those cases was similarly noncommunicative: "No such luck!" Again, no explanation.

But the answer I inwardly felt like giving was that any decent preacher who's already held forth on the propers for the day can do it again without mock heroics or fishing for compliments. In fact, all my life I've liked nothing better than to preach two or three times on a Sunday. By the third time I work my way through my notes, I've gotten sufficiently free of them to lose the irrelevant ones, make the good ones shine, and possibly even get the logic of the sermon right.

Bad habit number three (which is the same as number two but turns it into a blessing in disguise). Once again, what I'm about to say applies mostly to manuscript preachers. Since they don't ordinarily give equal preparation time to their "lesser" sermons, they settle for ten to twenty minutes' worth of jottings on an index card and then wing it. Yet the odd result (not always noticed by the preachers themselves but frequently by the more discerning in their flock) is that they preach better at eight than at ten. Deprived of their usual overblown beginnings — of the gingerbread-encrusted front porches they weary themselves to build — they go straight to the middle of what they have to say and often make a fair job of it. Best of all, when they've finished with the middle, they end the homily. Without dallying on a back porch to roam one more time through what they've already said, they just say, "In the Name of the Father, the Son, and the Holy Spirit," and let it go at that.

The lesson here is that when you've done the job you went to the pulpit to do, shut up. Don't keep hammering on the homiletical woodwork till you put half-moons all over it — not to mention your congregation. It's a lesson mostly lost on preachers whose sermons are all front porch and rear deck with no discernible house in between; but if you're committed to the house of faith, you may find it helpful. So my first piece of advice to you, whether you preach from notes or manuscript, is to forget about fabulous beginnings and compelling endings and spend almost all of your preparation time developing a meaty middle. Give the Word of God a break, for Christ's sake! Starting your sermon with anecdotes about your high-school gym teacher or your Aunt Helen's shopping habits is pre-empting the Word's time. Winding it up with a poem and a prayer is nattering on after he's stopped talking.

I have nothing against great beginnings and endings, but even the best preachers don't come up with many of them. The notion (sometimes encouraged by homiletics instructors) that every Tom, Dick, and Harriet has to have both in every sermon is a snare and a delusion. If you can come up with either, fine; but don't fritter away your precious time with your Friend in the House of Scripture by working too long on them beforehand. Windy beginnings, no matter how well-wrought, are just throat-clearing. Gassy endings, however satisfying to the preacher, seldom amount to much more than a belch. All they do is take up too much of your preparation time: your Friend doesn't have a prayer of getting anything else to come out of your mouth.

Now we're ready to talk about the production of your notes.

First step. On Monday morning (no later), read and reread *in the Bible itself* all the pericopes appointed in the Lectionary for the upcoming Sunday. If you have a Bible program in your computer, get up early and print them out with wide margins — and always include all the parts the Lectionary may have chopped out. The margins are to give you room for making preliminary notes, and the censored parts are put in to make room for the Word — no matter what anybody thinks he should or shouldn't have said. Then go back to your reading/rereading/listening; and only after that take the next step.

When you've got at least a clue about which reading (or readings) you'll be preaching on (and a clear, if general, notion of what you think you hear the Word saying to you in it or them), set up a *table* on your word-processing program (in *landscape* format, to give yourself wider columns) and put into it the full text of the passage(s) you've chosen (you can always trim later). This will be the document that will eventually contain your notes. It doesn't matter if your final version of them is done by hand or on the computer (though I frequently settle for just the Scripture text(s) in the computer version and fill in my notes in pencil — because a long set of notes, in table-format, can give you *agita* on the screen). By the way: if you're not a computer person, let me reassure you that you can do this whole job just as well with pencil and paper. If that was good enough for Augustine and Donne, it will certainly be good enough for you. Still, on the assumption that you can navigate your way through a Bible program and a word processor, here's a sample blank of the table format I myself happen to use, just in case you're interested. It's yours: feel free to do anything you like with it.

Day	Date	Your name	Sermon title	Pericope	Church name	Page number

BEGINNING: (11 pt. font, line spacing at exactly 16 pt., full justification)

ON:

Your *preaching notes* on the passage, to be positioned opposite the appropriate places in the text	The *text of your pericope*, from whatever version you've decided to use
Font: 11 pt.; line spacing at exactly 16 pt.; left or full justification	Font: 11 pt.; line spacing at exactly 16 pt., full justification
	Additional Scripture quotes, comments, illustrations, etc.
	Font: 11 pt.; line spacing at exactly 16 pt., left or full justification

ENDING: (11 pt. font, line spacing at exactly 16 pt., full justification)

The center column, depending on the length of your pericope, may run to several pages. If you've got bad eyes, you might set the characters at 12 points; if you've got good eyes, you might even set them at 10 or 9. I'll give you filled-in blanks showing specific sermons later in this chapter. When those appear, you'll notice that I don't bother to put in the grid-lines because they clutter things up in the pulpit. I've formatted them in here simply to show you the tabular arrangement at a glance. In any case, here's what one will look like preliminarily filled in — with a lesson text in the center column and plenty of room for penciling in notes on the sides.

In the Name of the Father, etc. Today, . . .

ON:

NRSV John 17:1 After Jesus had spoken these words, he looked up to heaven and said, "Father, the hour has come; glorify your Son so that the Son may glorify you, 2 since you have given him authority over all people, to give eternal life to all whom you have given him. 3 And this is eternal life, that they may know you, the only true God, and Jesus Christ whom you have sent. 4 I glorified you on earth by finishing the work that you gave me to do. 5 So now, Father, glorify me in your own presence with the glory that I had in your presence before . . .

THEREFORE. . . . . *In the Name of the Father, etc.*

Incidentally, the purpose of the line spacing at exactly 16 points (or even a few more, if you like) is to insure that your text — and your notes, if you do them on the computer — will be readable in the pulpit. It's also to insure that your notes will line up with your Scripture text, no matter how you may alter point sizes in the several columns. Best of all, though, once you've set up the table format, you'll never have to do it again. All you need to do to set up new preaching notes is bring up an old set and save it immediately under a new file name, such as 096PAS1.SRM, or 096LEN5.SRM. (Those are the names of my files for the Easter Day and 5 Lent sermon notes I'm going to show you shortly.) Then you delete the previous text in the "beginning" row, as well as the text in all the columns of the "middle" row(s) and in the "ending" row — and off you go to work on your next sermon.

Even more incidentally, when you first set up your table format, be sure to put into it at least ten (10) rows. One of the annoyances you can run into when you're working in columns that go on for several pages in a single row is that when you make deletions or insertions, they move everything below them up or down, thus knocking your already aligned text and notes out of place — and necessitating a lot of burdensome re-aligning. So whenever you see a page-break line come up on your screen, copy the two lines above the break (plus whatever's below it), move it all to the *next row,* and continue on your merry way. You'll thank me for this one: moving a few lines of typing to a new row is child's play compared with the *tsouris* of having to re-align four pages' worth of notes and text after you stuck a last-minute bright idea into page one. But back to your sermon-preparation schedule.

Second step. Having set things up on Monday, you spend Tuesday through Friday, as you have time (or make it), dealing with your pericope. For openers, take a good look at what comes before and after it in the book of the Bible in which it occurs. It's hard to overstress the importance of this exercise. If you don't do it, your experience as a preacher will probably lead you to the not-so-bright idea of preaching on what you've always assumed the passage was saying. Maybe you'll be right. But with luck, maybe you'll find you were wrong — and that for the first time you have a chance of hitting the bull's-eye instead of the barn. A thoughtful look at what precedes and follows a passage is the world's best way of getting a fresh view of it. Accordingly, ask yourself, "Why does this passage come here and not someplace else? What bee was in the bonnet of Jesus (or Paul, or whoever) before he said this? Where does he seem to have been planning to go next — and why?" This cross-examination of yourself can and must take time. There are books of the Bible (Jeremiah, for instance) in which only the Holy Spirit can figure out the logical connections between certain passages. In the New Testament, mercifully, the argument of the books is usually more penetrable, but not always. The Spirit has been frustratingly patient with editors anybody else would have fired. So look long and hard for answers to your questions. Above all, try to *hear* what's going on.

That done, go through the text in your table format, underline the appropriate words or phrases, and then scribble in the notes you've come up with — especially the fresh ones. But next, take another pass through the whole thing and try to hear some more freshness. Or, better said, in the words of Gerard Manley Hopkins' poem "Pied Beauty," try to hear things

> counter, original, spare, strange;
> > Whatever is fickle, freckled (who knows how?)
> > With swift, slow; sweet, sour; adazzle, dim . . .

Then start playing with your notes on the text. *Wrestle* with them — and with *it*. If it seems unwilling to succumb to your attempts to pin it down, take a pencil and another sheet of paper and write down your complaints against it. Forget for a while that you're supposed to be producing sermon notes here, and just bellyache. Sometimes a good cussing out clears the air, to say nothing of the mind. If *you* can't understand the text, your congregation probably won't, either. (You might even find yourself making

89

a few notes for your beginning or ending without knowing it; but because of the danger of derailing yourself, don't try to do anything conclusive about those parts of your sermon now.)

Then sweat. Look at your text in its table format long and long. Continue underlining, in pencil, the words and phrases that speak to you. Put question marks or exclamation points against the bits that don't seem to fit your sense of the thrust of the passage. Make more notes in the columns on either side of your text. But not in ink. This isn't the TV Guide crossword you're doing here; it's *The Times* of London puzzle. And don't make your notes on the computer now, either; if you do, they'll look so *finished* that they'll trick you into thinking you've got them set in stone. Always wait until Saturday before you even think of getting them out of their scribbled state and into the machine.

That's the way your week will go, Monday through Friday — with time off, perhaps, for good behavior and the inevitable time out for your parishioners' misbehavior. The exact days and times you'll work on your notes during the week will depend on your schedule — and your temperament. The world is divided neatly between morning people and night people. Depending on which you are, you can either get up earlier, or stay up later, and do your work then. Five-thirty in the morning and eleven-thirty at night are the only times at which your phone won't ring (unless you've trained your parish to plague you at all hours — in which case you have a bigger problem than any preaching book can help you with). Just remember: you do indeed have other obligations; but you don't have a bigger one than this. *Attend* to it, devoutly.

On Friday, write down your preliminary notes for the *beginning* and the *ending* of your sermon. I'll give you more on this subject in the next chapter when I have my say about written-out sermons. Here, I have just two rules for navigating these dangerous waters.

Rule one is something I've said more than once already: Never even attempt to compose the start or finish of your sermon until you've spent many days working on the all-important middle. Good writers almost never produce the beginnings that get published in their books at the beginning of their labors. Instead, they get themselves rolling with whatever stuff and nonsense they can come up with, and only at the end of their work do they go back and seriously tackle the problem of getting started. A casual reader may assume that he or she is enjoying what the author first thought of; but unless the writer is a genius (or lucky), any start that's written on the first sprint almost always needs at least a course correction after the finish line's been crossed. So to save yourself that trouble, do this: write your notes for the ending of your sermon right after you're done with those for the middle, and only then — when you know what you've said and where you came out — make your notes for the beginning.

Rule two: Keep them short. You've spent all your time until now on the middle of your sermon — on the *meat* of it. Don't bracket the bountiful meal you're going to serve with plattersful of appetizers for the cocktail hour and uranium-density chocolate bombes for dessert. When you do come to put your salutatory and valedictory notes into the computer table-format I've suggested, you'll be in *Landscape* orientation (and in a single column), so you'll have the full width of the page for them: *two lines only* are a good maximum to set for the notes that will get you into and out of your sermon. If you find you run over, prune them back ruthlessly until they consist of no more than key words and phrases you can fit inside that limit. (You'll find that I myself violate this limit as often as I keep to it. But both your listeners and the Holy Spirit will thank you for your brevity.)

Third step. You come now to Saturday. You've spent four (?) days getting your mind and your notes in order: finally, it's time to produce something you can use. At this juncture, you'd do well to remember another home truth — this one about the creative process: No work of art (at least as far as the artist is concerned) is ever finished; he or she simply abandons it. The great ones, obviously, achieve that abandonment at a high level: Bach stopped working on the *Toccata and Fugue in d minor* at a level of excellence that Telemann never reached; Marianne Moore left off her writing of the poem *Poetry* where the foot of Eddie Guest never trod. They just gave up and got their work out. They didn't spend an eternity fiddling with it.

Hence your Saturday labors: produce, on the computer (or by hand), the fairest copy of your notes that you can manage. If you entered them on the computer, print out a draft to see what your preaching copy will look like. Then sit down with your notes, away from the computer, take a pencil — and edit, revise, and emend to your heart's content, one last time. Then go back to the computer, punch in your changes, print a couple of final copies — and kiss the machine good-bye for the week. Mow the lawn, watch football on TV, or have a beer; but don't look at your sermon notes again until Sunday morning. You've done what you could. It's time to trust God to do the rest.

Fourth and last step. You come to Sunday. Get up in the dark — and not just because you need to give yourself time. Principally, it's to remind yourself that whether you've prepared well or badly, that's exactly where you are: you're waiting in darkness for your Friend to give you whatever he decides. Sit down to your notes with a pencil and a highlighter. Your purpose now is not to improve on your notes but to get them, as they are, into your bloodstream. Highlight (sparingly) the notes you want to jump out at you in the pulpit. Talk your way through them. Get a feel for the thrust of your sermon. Pencil in stars next to points that now strike you as central. Draw arrows to things you now think you want to hit before you get to the next thing in your notes as they stand. In other words, keep talking and scribbling through them — even until your fair copy isn't fair anymore.

Remember this above all. Get your notes down pat; make them so thoroughly a part of you that you'll hardly need them when you preach. A note preacher is a raconteur, not a reader or a reciter of memorized jottings. Your notes are not a manuscript giving you the ipsissima verba of your sermon; they're a prompter who's going to whisper to you, "Now tell them the one about . . ." By the time you preach from your notes, your sermon ought to come out as off-handedly as a string of old jokes — with no more stilt or stuff-iness to it than the story about MacTavish and the Kilt. Stay with them early on Sunday morning, then, until they're second nature to you. The fact that they get messy is not important: if you've done your final run-through of your notes properly, you'll barely look at them in the pulpit.

One more — and crucial — comment: If all of a sudden you find yourself tempted to turn your sermon onto a totally new track as the result of something that comes to you then and there, give in to the temptation. At last, you're hot! You've spent a week getting ready for just this moment. Before now, you never had all the pieces in place. But here, in you, on this Sunday, God finally has a furnished mind to work with. So listen to his decorating advice, even if you have to throw out all the sofas and chairs you've taken six days to accumulate. Never mind that it will make a mess of your notes: if it's a powerful idea, it will be sufficiently in your ears now to shout itself out when you get into the pulpit. Once again, though: whatever you do, don't go back to the computer to pretty up the miserable things. Just send yourself to the showers — and go to church.

"To the showers." The phrase is apt: at last, you're off the field of your responsibility for the sermon. You're out of all the crowd-pleasing and overachieving that may have motivated you through your practice sessions. You're hanging out in the locker room, waiting for the Coach to change his mind and bring you back into the game. You might, I suppose, take a sneak peek at your notes during a quiet moment (if you ever get one) before the service; but it's not a great idea. It leads to panic, because it throws you back into wondering whether your notes are hopeless. Just remember that it's not up to you anymore. This is your day off.

I've always felt that way about Sundays. If I'm not ready by the time I walk to the pulpit, it's too late to worry about it. Whatever happens next will happen without fail — and without incident to Jesus' apple cart, even if it's a church fire that burns me to a crisp. I've done my part of the job; the rest is in God's hands. But since that would be the case even if I'd done nothing, I'm still home free. As Tom Lehrer sardonically put it,

> Once the rockets are up, who cares where they come down?
> That's not my department, says Werner von Braun.

Wiseacres sometimes say to preachers, "You guys are lucky; you only work one day a week." My answer to that one has always been, "No, I don't. And I don't work Monday through Saturday, either. I get paid for hanging around." Try it; it's not a bad answer. It wouldn't hurt them to meet at least one person who's *free*.

Oh, one more thing. If you're dying to clean up your sermon notes for posterity, don't do it until after you've preached — and do it on Sunday afternoon, as a penance for your vanity.

*   *   *

The last item on the agenda for this chapter will be two examples of my own notes for sermons I've preached recently. Let me preface them with a few remarks.

As I said, I prepared them while I was writing this book. The shorter set was for a sermon on the Second Reading for Easter Day, Year A; the other was on the Gospel for the Fifth Sunday in Lent two weeks earlier. The notes I preached on in Lent turned into a very long sermon indeed (over thirty minutes) — about which someone said to me, "After such a long Gospel, how can you get so much pleasure out of adding insult to injury?" Perhaps in response to that, my notes for the Easter sermon were considerably shorter.

You'll notice that I use several typographical devices for calling my own attention to things I especially want to emphasize when I'm preaching. I <u>underline</u> key words and phrases in the texts from Scripture; for example: Εἰ οὖν <u>συνηγέρθητε</u> τῷ Χριστῷ, τὰ ἄνω <u>ζητεῖτε</u>. I use Capital Letters to alert myself to what I think is KEY MATE-RIAL in the notes; and I use <u>double underlines</u> under CAPS within

94

[square brackets] to clue myself in (by title only) to my [ILLUSTRA-
TIONS]. (That may strike you as a fuss to type, but you can always
customize a button-bar command to execute the double underlin-
ing. It's not a chore.) Finally, I use arrows ($\downarrow \rightarrow \uparrow \leftarrow$) to remind
myself to switch to a different column while I'm preaching. (In the
text as you'll see it printed out, they represent the arrows I penciled
in at the last minute before giving the sermon.)

In my notes, I normally print the texts of New Testament
lessons in Greek because I read it well enough to be able to do a
kind of simultaneous translation at sight. The notes for the Easter
sermon have been left that way; but in the notes for the fifth Sunday
in Lent, I've taken out the Greek and put in the NRSV, just to show
that it can be done any way you like.

Lastly, as you know, I don't always follow my own advice. The
beginning of the 5 Lent sermon turned out to be a monster of a
front porch because (wisely or unwisely) I decided not only to
recapitulate the Gospels for the two previous Sundays and to note
the parallels between the Raising of Lazarus and Ezekiel's Valley
of Dry Bones, but also to take yet another crack at the Mystery of
Christ that underlies all those scriptural passages. I've tried to cut
them back for this book, but it does sometimes seem as if my
porches are asking for equal billing with the house.

Anyway, with no more apologies or throat-clearing, here they
are.

EASTER: (Congregation still standing; teach): **V:** Χριστός ἀνέστη. **R:** Ἀληθῶς ἀνέστη. *In Nomine Patris, etc.* JESUS your LIFE is HIDDEN in your DEATH. And he's hidden there RIGHT NOW — NOT in a FUTURE resurrection a week from some Tuesday.

BEGIN: ↓↓↓

You've ALREADY BEEN RAISED. Your resurrection was proclaimed over you in BAPTISM; but it was THERE BEFORE — since your CONCEPTION, and since the FOUNDATION OF THE WORLD. JESUS, our BEGINNING AND OUR END, has always been PRESENT IN EVERY NOW. That's what the SACRAMENTS are all about: IT'S ALL DONE. HE'S ALWAYS been here in the POWER OF HIS RESURRECTION. We've always been [SITTING] with him.
→↑

↓
Colossians 3:1 Εἰ οὖν συνηγέρθητε τῷ Χριστῷ, τὰ ἄνω ζητεῖτε, οὗ ὁ Χριστός ἐστιν ἐν δεξιᾷ τοῦ θεοῦ καθήμενος· 2 τὰ ἄνω φρονεῖτε, μὴ τὰ ἐπὶ τῆς γῆς.

τὰ ἄνω ... καθήμενος· [SITTING] together with Christ in the heavenly places (Eph. 2:6). The joy of Easter is the joy of the final [PARTY] already PRESENT in us NOW by the Mystery of Christ! Don't try to GET A LIFE here on earth. [SUCCESS / CONTROL]. Don't FEAR DEATH. We spend so much time fearing, fighting death [SMOKING / BEING BORN IS THE MAJOR CAUSE OF DYING]. But it's ALREADY OVER: We already HAVE A LIFE in the LAND of the TRINITY — TRUST it NOW, ENJOY it NOW!

BECAUSE you're ALREADY DEAD, and your LIFE is HIDDEN in JESUS — in the MYSTERY of CHRIST. WE'RE [FREE!!!]. THERE IS THEREFORE NOW NO CONDEMNATION — HE MAKES IT ALL HAPPEN. HE'S AL-WAYS PRESENT.

3 ἀπεθάνετε γὰρ καὶ ἡ ζωὴ ὑμῶν κέκρυπται σὺν τῷ Χριστῷ ἐν τῷ θεῷ· 4 ὅταν ὁ Χριστὸς φανερωθῇ, ἡ ζωὴ ὑμῶν, τότε καὶ ὑμεῖς σὺν αὐτῷ φανερωθήσεσθε ἐν δόξῃ.

ἀπεθάνετε κέκρυπται φανερωθῇ ζωὴ φανερωθήσεσθε: The only difference between US and the DEAD is that they now SEE FACE TO FACE what we can only TRUST. But WE ALL HAVE IT NOW, FULLY!

THEREFORE: We REJOICE IN OUR RESURRECTION not because it's COMING, or because it's a JOB we have to COOPERATE WITH, but because IT'S ALREADY A FACT. So TRUST! LIVE IN THE FREEDOM OF YOUR FAITH! THE SUNNY SIDE OF THE STREET!   *In Nomine Patris, etc.*

Just a couple of comments on this first sermon. My [IL-LUSTRATIONS] may strike you as being cryptic to the point of unintelligibility: here's a little explanation of each of them.

Verse 1: [SITTING], [PARTY]: The passage in the back of my mind was Ephesians 2:5-6: ". . . while we were dead in our trespasses he made us alive together with Christ — by Grace you are saved — and he raised us up together with him, and made us sit together in the heavenly places in Christ Jesus. . . ." The New Testament is full of relaxing imagery, party imagery. Jesus did his first "sign" at a wedding reception; he spent many hours freeloading at other people's dinner parties; and at the end, in Revelation 19, there is the endless bash of the marriage Supper of the Lamb. That final party is the biggest fact of our lives — and it's the one fact that's going to last as long as we will in the hands of Jesus. Its truths are the only truths about us that count. If you and your brother-in-law are now on the outs with each other — even if you hate each other and haven't spoken for twenty years — in that very same now, you are reconciled in Jesus (accepted in the Beloved), and the two of you are sitting at the heavenly wedding reception, hoisting a cheerful glass in honor of the Bride and Groom.

Verse 2: [SUCCESS/CONTROL]: "Get a life!" we tell everybody. But that's a recipe for disaster. It's our very efforts at "getting a life" — at controlling everything and everybody around us (ourselves included) — that have made us the messes we are. We clutch at control, but life is radically beyond our control. You have no guarantee (you never did have and you never will) that tomorrow the corner of a building won't fall on you, or that your kids won't end up in jail, or that your biopsy won't come back positive.

Same verse: [SMOKING/BEING BORN IS THE MAJOR CAUSE OF DYING]: The promise in all the hoo-ha about not smoking isn't health. It's put that way, to be sure. But the smoke police — and the media biddies (of both sexes) who regale you with statistical horror stories about the evils of tobacco — have something far more sweeping in mind. Their actual promise, if you read the fine print, is that you won't die. Yet you know better: getting

98

born is the most terminal disease of all. And the same thing goes for the promises in all the diet-mongering, exercise-peddling, pseudo-eastern New Age spirituality that's floating around in your environment. You can do it all as religiously as you like, and you'll end up "six feet under" just the same — even in a columbarium. If you're trying to avoid death, you've lost the game already: your fatal mistake was going along with your mother's delivery of you. (Job 3:12: "Why were there knees to receive me, or breasts for me to suck?")

Verses 3-4: [FREE!!!]: You are delivered, now and forever, from the tiresome business of having to get a life for yourself because in Jesus, God has taken away all the garbage you accumulated by trying to save your life and handed you a free life in the losing of his Beloved Son. As he holds you in Jesus, all your labor, all your controlling, all your bookkeeping is over. You're dead! Not mortified, not embarrassed, not in Dutch; not arrested, not indicted, not on trial, not condemned. You're a corpse that the life-enhancement feds can't touch. There's nothing for you to do; it's all a gift. If you trusted it, it would make you happy: you would know Jesus' truth about you, and that truth would make you free. Still, even if you don't trust, you remain free. You have the freedom of his acceptance anyway, whether you want it or not. You can't get away from the Love that will not let you go.

On to the next sermon:

In Nomine Patris, etc. GOSPEL: THE RAISING OF LAZARUS. TIE IN past 2 Sundays: WOMAN AT WELL & MAN BORN BLIND. The MYSTERY of how God RUNS the world in the LOSERS of the world; how he MANAGES HISTORY through DEATH by the INCARNATION OF HIS WORD in human nature. The JOB is not just for a SELECT FEW, or done at a SINGLE TIME back in Palestine. It's his CONSTANT PRESENCE IN EVERYBODY from start to finish. JESUS is not the SOLE OCCURRENCE of the JOB; he's the GREAT SACRAMENT of it — and it's a MYSTERY because it's HIDDEN in all the LOSING of the world (WOMAN, BLIND MAN) — in the LAST, the LOST, the LEAST, the LITTLE, and the DEAD.

But today, in LAZARUS, we see it in a SUPREME LOSER — in a CORPSE. Easter's coming, yes; but don't move TOO FAST from death to resurrection. HOLY WEEK holds us in HIS death and OURS. JESUS came to RAISE THE DEAD, and ONLY THE DEAD. DEATH is our only PERSONAL EVIDENCE OF THE RESURRECTION. 2 NOTES *before we begin:*

First, *EZEKIEL: VALLEY OF DRY BONES = DEATH. The MYSTERY of the Incarnate Word in the OT. This Resurrection of bones ≠ just GETTING BACK into OLD SHAPE: Flesh, sinews, etc. reappear on bones; but THEY HAVE NO LIFE until the BREATH comes into them. They only WAIT IN FAITH until the SPIRIT WHO "TAKES of what is CHRIST'S and PROCLAIMS it to us" comes into them.*

Second, *GOSPEL: John PLACES the raising of LAZARUS (as Matthew does the Great Judgment parable) right before the PASSION NARRATIVE. And both put those passages there for the SAME REASON the church puts Lent before Easter: to underscore the SOLE NECESSITY OF FAITH in the MYSTERY of Jesus in our DEATHS.*

ON ↓↓↓

NRSV John 11:1 Now a certain man was ill, Lazarus of Bethany, the village of Mary and her sister Martha. 2 Mary was the one who anointed the Lord with perfume and wiped his feet with her

Mary did this for Jesus' BURIAL back then; in this episode, she becomes the only one who TRUSTS him in his DEATH.

hair; her brother Lazarus was ill. 3 So the sisters sent a message to Jesus, "Lord, he whom you love is ill."

4 But when Jesus heard it, he said, "This illness does not lead to death; rather it is for God's glory, so that the Son of God may be glorified through it."

5 Accordingly, though Jesus loved Martha and her sister and Lazarus, 6 after having heard that Lazarus was ill, he stayed two days longer in the place where he was. 7 Then after this he said to the disciples, "Let us go to Judea again." 8 The disciples said to him, "Rabbi, the Jews were just now trying to stone you, and are you going there again?" 9 Jesus answered, "Are there not twelve hours of daylight? Those who walk during the day do not stumble, because they see the light of this world. 10 But those who walk at night stumble, because the light is not in them." 11 After saying this, he told them, "Our friend Lazarus has fallen asleep, but I am going there to awaken him." 12 The disciples said to him, "Lord, if he has fallen asleep, he will be all right." 13 Jesus, however, had been speaking about his death, but they thought that he was referring merely to sleep. 14 Then Jesus told them plainly, "Lazarus is dead."

SICKNESS, WEAKNESS — LOSERS as God's cup of tea. [HOSPITAL PATIENTS VS. DOCTORS AS ICONS OF JESUS].

Parallel to BLIND MAN, John 9: " ... that the works of God might be made manifest through Lazarus' WEAKNESS [ασθένια]." This isn't about LAZARUS' death; it's about JESUS going to death itself so he might reveal the GLORY of the Mystery IN DEATH.

Jesus deliberately stays away; but now he's ready to go.

BLIND MAN again: [NIGHT / DAY]. Jesus first refers to the SUN; but he segues into "the LIGHT that shines in the darkness." We find Jesus in the [DARKNESS].

The disciples MISUNDERSTAND him: Jesus tells them Lazarus is RESTING: the verb κεκοίμηται is used for both "lying down" and "dying"; but Jesus corrects the disciples PLAINLY. The whole episode is about FAITH. But they don't have even a suspicion of the MYSTERY, can't see beyond the PLCT to kill Jesus. They SPEAK the TRUTH,

15 For your sake I am glad I was not there, so that you may believe. But let us go to him." 16 Thomas, who was called the Twin, said to his fellow disciples, "Let us also go, that we may die with him."

but they don't really BELIEVE. [THOMAS / CAIAPHAS].

21 Martha said to Jesus, "Lord, if you had been here, my brother would not have died. 22 But even now I know that God will give you whatever you ask of him."

Martha has a KIND OF FAITH. She trusts Jesus, but only as a LEFT-BRAINED person does. Her FASCINATION with CONTROL keeps her from going all the way. [THE TREE OF THE KNOWLEDGE OF GOOD AND EVIL]. Only God can decide WHO SHALL LIVE AND WHO SHALL DIE. Martha's view of the MESSIAH is that he'll INTERFERE in the MANAGEMENT of the world; but God LETS IT BE, as in CREATION. Jesus doesn't INTERFERE; he just takes the system's lumps and drops the subject of the Knowledge *of* Good & Evil down into the DARKNESS of his death. Hence her confusion.

23 Jesus said to her, "Your brother will rise again." 24 Martha said to him, "I know that he will rise again in the resurrection on the last day."

Martha's still stuck in KNOWING: she simply parrots her old [PHARISEE SUNDAY SCHOOL LESSON].

25 Jesus said to her, "I am the resurrection and the life. Those who believe in me, even though they die, will live, 26 and everyone who lives and believes in me will never die. Do you

This is entirely about JESUS, not some MIRACLE or some WIDGET. Jesus IS the Resurrection; he doesn't just DO resurrections. FAITH again: in the MYSTERY, everybody rises (the "Resurrection of the Just and the Unjust").

believe this?" 27 She said to him, "Yes, Lord, I believe that you are the Messiah, the Son of God, the one coming into the world."

28 When she had said this, she went back and called her sister Mary, and told her privately, "The Teacher is here and is calling for you." 29 And when she heard it, she got up quickly and went to him. 30 Now Jesus had not yet come to the village, but was still at the place where Martha had met him. 31 The Jews who were with her in the house, consoling her, saw Mary get up quickly and go out. They followed her because they thought that she was going to the tomb to weep there.

32 When Mary came where Jesus was and saw him, she knelt at his feet and said to him, "Lord, if you had been here, my brother would not have died."

Mary's ADORATION. She repeats Martha's words, but with a difference: Martha talks about how the Messiah should MANAGE the World; but Mary enters HIS PASSION BY HER PASSION.

33 When Jesus saw her weeping, and the Jews who came with her also weeping, he was greatly disturbed in spirit and deeply moved.

(TEARS, again). Jesus is GROANING (ἐνεβριμήσατο τῷ πνεύματι). He's upset, angry, pissed off, at the MIS-UNDERSTANDINGS that inevitably follow from the SIGNS he gives to elicit only FAITH. And the MOURNERS MIS-READ HIS WEEPING as mere, helpless FONDNESS.

34 He said, "Where have you laid him?" They said to him, "Lord, come and see." 35 Jesus began to weep. 36 So the

Jews said, "See how he loved him!" 37 But some of them said, "Could not he who opened the eyes of the blind man have kept this man from dying?"

38 Then <u>Jesus</u>, again <u>greatly disturbed</u>, came to the tomb. It was a cave, and a stone was lying against it. 39 Jesus said, "Take away the stone." <u>Martha</u>, the sister of the dead man, said to him, "Lord, already there is a stench because he has been dead four days." 40 <u>Jesus</u> said to her, "Did I not tell you that if you <u>believed</u>, you would see the glory of God?"

41 So they took away the stone. And <u>Jesus looked upward</u> and said, "<u>Father, I thank you</u> for having heard me. 42 I knew that you always hear me, but I have said this for the sake of the crowd standing here, so that they may believe that you sent me." 43 When he had said this, he cried with a loud voice, "<u>Lazarus, come out!</u>" 44 The dead man came out, his hands and feet bound with strips of cloth, and his face wrapped in a cloth. Jesus said to them, "<u>Unbind him, and let him go.</u>"

Same word, same ANGER.

This is not just about getting her brother back; it's about TRUSTING THE MYSTERY.

JESUS' PRAYER: *THEY TAKE AWAY* the stone; *HE* TAKES his eyes *AWAY* from the mere TRANSACTION of raising a corpse to CONTEMPLATE THE MYSTERY. He thanks the Father, RELAXING into the Mystery: he knows, feels, is CONFIDENT that he and the Father are one. He has no doubts that the TRANSACTION of raising Lazarus will come off; but he knows that its only real purpose is to reveal HIMSELF as the PRESENCE OF THE MYSTERY so they might BELIEVE. And so it happens: Lazarus isn't LOOSED into a MERE RESUMPTION of his old life; he never got that back: <u>[THE PLOT TO KILL LAZARUS / THANKS A LOT, JESUS]</u>; he's RELEASED into the LIBERATION of the MYSTERY that has always lain at the

104

roots of his being — and IN HIM, at the ROOTS OF THE BE-ING OF EVERYTHING AND EVERYBODY. [RESURREC-TION AS A COSMIC DISPENSATION].

THEREFORE: ALL WE NEED TO DO IS TRUST HIM IN OUR DEATH. Like MARTHA, we may TRUST HIM SHAKILY; or like MARY, we may TRUST HIM FULLY — even with TEARS at the SAD, TERRIBLE LOVE that raises us up out of DEATH. But whichever one we may be, EVERY LAST ONE OF US, and EVERY LAST CHILD OF ADAM AND EVE, will be raised like LAZARUS. ONCE AGAIN, the only thing that counts to him is our death. DEATH is the only TICKET we NEED. JESUS DOES ALL THE REST.   *In Nomine Patris, etc.*

Those notes, obviously, were in the exegetical/expository vein. In addition, because of the length of the Gospel, it took a fair amount of time to preach the sermon from them. Which brings us to the subject of the length of sermons. When people complain to me that I preached too long — or when they ask me (leadingly) how long I think a sermon should be — I have some more stock replies. To the carpers, I say, "Well, tell me what I said that was off the subject. Was it something other than the length of my sermon that tried your patience? As far as I know, there aren't any biblical pronouncements about the amount of time a preacher is allotted; there are only the habitual assumptions of churchgoers. Tell me what was wrong substantively, not what made you fidget with your watch." (Sometimes this approach nets me a little insight into preaching better, but most of the time it just annoys the hell out of them. Either way, though, somebody benefits.) But to the others, all I say is, "A good sermon is one that's long enough to go from its beginning to its end without passing through anything but its own middle. That's what I aim for. If I didn't hit the mark today, tell me where my aim was off."

Comments on the [ILLUSTRATIONS]:

Verses 2-3: [HOSPITAL PATIENTS VS. DOCTORS AS ICONS OF JESUS]: The patients on their beds of pain look more like Jesus on the cross than the doctors with their stethoscopes and white coats. In the parable of The Good Samaritan, it's the man half-dead on the ground who's the Christ figure, not the Samaritan. The Samaritan is just one of three stick-figures (along with the Priest and the Levite) whom Jesus introduces to define "neighbor" for the lawyer — and for you. Your neighbors are all the Losers in the world, because they're the ones who are the sacraments of the Mystery of Christ. (Remember the parable of The Great Judgment in Matthew 25:31-46? Everybody in it is a loser — including the King, since he languished hungry, thirsty, a stranger, naked, sick, and in prison while the goats were busy getting a life for themselves.)

Verses 9-10: [NIGHT] [DARKNESS]: God in Christ works in

the dark. The Light of the incarnate Word shines in the darkness; Nicodemus comes to Jesus at night; Jesus gives sight to the blind; his Passion begins on a dark night in the Garden of Gethsemane; the sky is darkened at his crucifixion; he himself goes dark at his death; and he lies in the blackness of the tomb. I want you to note a supremely important point here: *Jesus is in the darkness forever.* If God in Christ is dead for even five minutes, those five minutes are held forever in the bosom of the Trinity. Jesus' death is as eternal as his life in the resurrection. He doesn't just take a three-day nap in the tomb and then come blithely out, ignoring the subject of death like some transmigration-of-souls guru. By the fact that he's God, he has those three dead days eternally present in himself. And when he comes to us in our deaths, he brings us into his death before he lifts us into his resurrection. As his death is the historical sacrament, the real presence, of the new creation, so our death is our personal sacrament of that same reconciled order. It's something we're supposed to celebrate, not take the edge off with pipe dreams of immortality. Death is the choicest piece of evidence we have for our resurrection.

Verse 16: [THOMAS/CAIAPHAS]: Thomas, like Caiaphas, speaks the truth without knowing it. But also like him, Thomas at this point is very far from the truth personally — and like both of them, we're the same way. We fence with death: we try to dodge its rapier. We may think about it, or babble on about it, or fear it for ourselves, or inflict it on others — but we can't rejoice in it because we won't trust that it's the presence of God to us. Thomas has a long way to go before he can do that. True enough, Jesus' words to Peter in John 21:18-19 will sooner or later apply to him (and to us): "'When you were young, you girded yourself . . . but when you're old . . . another will gird you and carry you where you don't want to go.' This he said, signifying [σημαίνων, "signaling"] by what death he [meaning Peter — and Thomas, and you, and me] would glorify God." But he's not there yet.

Verse 21: [THE TREE OF THE KNOWLEDGE OF GOOD AND EVIL]: Because my congregation had heard me do this subject in other sermons, I did a quick take on it (along the lines of what I said to you back in Chapter Three when I gave you Daniel Quinn's theory about the passage).

Verses 23-24: [PHARISEE SUNDAY SCHOOL LESSON]: Martha, Mary, and Lazarus (and probably Jesus) seem to have been raised with an awareness of the pharisaic doctrine of a general resurrection at the last day. I paraphrased what F. D. Maurice once said about the church's track record for getting the resurrection wrong. I said something like this: After two thousand years, the church hasn't gotten Christians any further than the Pharisees got Martha. We still think the resurrection won't happen until the last day (even though in baptism, we're proclaimed resurrected right now); and we still think the resurrection is a reward for select types who behave themselves (even though it's a cosmic gift to everybody who can manage to end up dead).

Verses 25-26: [WIDGET]: (Same thing: The resurrection is not a gadget, not a transactional device that bestows on us something we didn't have before. Everybody in the world is risen in Jesus: believer or non-believer; good, bad, or indifferent. We don't *get* raised; we *are* risen, now!

Verses 43-44: [THE PLOT TO KILL LAZARUS/THANKS A LOT, JESUS]: Quite often, the help Jesus gives people is no favor to them. The Blind Man gets his sight back, but he's hassled by the Pharisees; Lazarus rises from the dead, but he dies again another day. (And in the meantime, because they consider him a menace too, the authorities hatch a plot to kill him as well as Jesus.)

Same verse: [RESURRECTION AS A COSMIC DISPENSA-TION]: A repeat of something I covered earlier on in the sermon. As I recall, I skipped this when I realized I'd already done it.

*   *   *

One last note: a word of realism about the admittedly rigorous note-preparation schedule I gave you for Monday through Friday. Hacking on the computer to get this chapter in order has kept me so busy that I haven't yet (today is Friday) done a thing about my sermon notes for Sunday. These things happen. I did get up early on Monday and put the Gospel for 2 Easter into table format; but I'm not going to be able to do anything about working on it until tomorrow. I tell you that for your comfort. Aim high and fall on your face: if it was good enough for Jesus, it's good enough for us.

TEN

Preaching from a Manuscript

For this chapter, I'm going to reverse the procedure I used in the last one. Instead of giving you general advice before practical examples, I'll start here with the examples, then give you the advice.

First, though, a touch of background on those examples. It's now the Monday after the Second Sunday of Easter. I spent so much time writing and banging on the computer last week that I ended up having to do almost all the work on my notes for 2 Easter early Saturday morning. When I got down to it, however, I had a pleasant surprise: I'd forgotten that I hadn't just printed out the Gospel text in table format last Monday; I'd penciled in fairly extensive notes on it. Better yet, at one of the two points where John says that Jesus came to the disciples when the doors were shut and stood in the midst of them (without any miraculous hocus-pocus about oozing his way through solid wood), I'd written down, "Theme: Our Closed Doors; Jesus as the Open Door." Best of all, I'd done a search through the New Testament on "door" (.θυρ*), printed it out, and made jottings on the printout. That meant I'd already put in about three hours on my notes. Three more hours of punching them into the computer and editing them into preachable shape would do the trick.

Three plus three equals six: that was the total time devoted to my notes last week before I sat down on Sunday at 4:00 A.M. with my pencil and highlighter. Nevertheless, something else about

110

my sermon-preparation routine might interest you. My wife, Valerie, and I have added a new wrinkle to the quasi-monastic life we live here on Shelter Island. Ever since I left the parish ministry in early February of 1996, we've mostly celebrated the Eucharist at home on Sundays. In the course of that exercise, I've gotten into the habit of preaching a sermon to her and whoever might be in the house as overnight company. Better yet, if I'm going to be on the road lecturing and have to preach in my host's church, I give her the sermon for that Sunday on the nearest previous Saturday. Last Saturday, accordingly (I had to preach yesterday at Christ Church, Sag Harbor), I did a run-through, out loud and in full, on the 2 Easter notes I propose to show you. As always, I got the benefit of Valerie's criticisms, reflections, insights — and her inevitable free advice.

It occurs to me you might profitably do something like that. Since it took me forty-seven years to discover this routine, it might even save you a little time. If you have a spouse who's willing to sit and listen, you could do what I do. But if you don't, why not try a variation on it? Why don't you schedule a Saturday Eucharist at the church and tell your parish you'll be working your way through Sunday's sermon? Or perhaps you could schedule a different kind of gathering. (You could call it a "Bible-study Session," or "The Pastor's Saturday Morning Kaffeeklatsch" — I've known preachers who've done that.) Whatever you call it, though, ask some friends you consider discerning to show up and help you out with their comments. Just make sure they know what you're up to — and that you've gotten your notes for the sermon up to weekend snuff. Who knows? They might be enthusiastic, or even feel honored. You're inviting them to make the preaching in their church more than a one-way street!

In any case, that's what I did this past Saturday — with the result that when I got to my desk on Sunday morning at 4:00 A.M. for the final talk-out and scribble-through of my notes, I came to them armed with the results of the discussion that Valerie and I had had about my sermon. It was as good as having to preach twice on the same day, but with more time to make repairs after the first time through. I was able to highlight, draw arrows, and circle things far more cannily than I would have without our Saturday session. Yesterday morning, accordingly, after about two hours of pounding my notes into my head, I sent myself to the showers, dressed, and went to church. The only dictum I didn't follow was the one about not going back to the computer: early on, I went back to it one more time, made two or three corrections, and printed out a new copy to work on. Apart from that, I took all my own advice: I never again looked at the notes before I preached; I put in my usual "corpse" time during the hymn before the Gospel; and then I let the sermon happen. (I don't think I looked at my notes more than a handful of times while I was preaching.) Grand Total, then, for last week's sermon preparation: 3 + 3 + 2 = 8 hours. Respectable enough, but hardly overwhelming.

Back to the business of this chapter. I have three items on the agenda.

First. I'm going to give you (without comment) my notes for yesterday's sermon as I tidied them up for the book this morning. (You're my posterity: I'm not about to appear before you unkempt and uncombed.)

Second. Since this is a chapter (believe it or not) on preaching from a manuscript, I shall give you that same sermon in full as if I were going to preach it without once departing from the printed text.

Third. After that, we'll get around to having a chat about the trials and tribulations (and with luck, the joys) of writing a sermon.

In Nomine Patris, etc.   On 2 ELEMENTS in the Gospel we just read. 1: The APPEARANCES of the Risen Jesus — Easter night / one week later — Jesus appears to the disciples despite LOCKED, CLOSED, DOORS; 2: NT IMAGERY of DOOR; Three repetitions of "PEACE."

ON: ↓↓↓

[APPEARANCES] [DOORS / DOOR] The SHUT DOORS (κλει = locked) and the OPEN DOOR (Jesus) NT IMAGERY OF DOOR. (3rd column)→

SHUT DOORS = The DOORS of OUR LIFE. We try to get a life by OPENING DOORS, but ALL THE DOORS of our plausible, sensible attempts to GET A LIFE will CLOSE. [EXPECTATIONS of HOPE]: Birth (first attempt at closed door); then Childhood; Adolescence; Marriage; Career; Stress; Sins; Illness; Loss; Grief; DEATH.

OPEN DOOR = JESUS, who is HIMSELF the DOOR. By his DEATH in OUR DEATHS, we have Jesus IN OUR MIDST, EVEN INSIDE THE CLOSED DOORS OF OUR LIVES.
→

GNT John 20:19 Οὔσης οὖν ὀψίας τῇ ἡμέρᾳ ἐκείνῃ τῇ μιᾷ σαββάτων καὶ τῶν θυρῶν κεκλεισμένων ὅπου ἦσαν οἱ μαθηταὶ διὰ τὸν φόβον τῶν Ἰουδαίων, ἦλθεν ὁ Ἰησοῦς καὶ ἔστη εἰς τὸ μέσον καὶ λέγει αὐτοῖς, Εἰρήνη ὑμῖν.

20 καὶ τοῦτο εἰπὼν ἔδειξεν τὰς χεῖρας καὶ τὴν πλευρὰν αὐτοῖς. ἐχάρησαν οὖν οἱ μαθηταὶ ἰδόντες τὸν κύριον. 21 εἶπεν οὖν αὐτοῖς [ὁ Ἰησοῦς] πάλιν, Εἰρήνη ὑμῖν. καθὼς ἀπέσταλκέν με ὁ πατήρ, κἀγὼ πέμπω ὑμᾶς.
↑

SEARCH ON DOOR
John 10:2: "I am the DOOR of the SHEEP" ("Go in and out and find pasture").

10:7, 9: "I am the DOOR" ("By ME, if anyone goes in and out ... SAVED").

Revelation 3:20: "Behold I stand [ἕστηκα, perfect tense] at the DOOR and knock; if anyone HEARS my VOICE ["my sheep hear "my voice"] and opens to me, I will come into his house and I WILL EAT [δειπνήσω] with HIM and HE WILL EAT with ME." [SUPPER /PARTY] (at END).

THOMAS: The DOOR of his MIND is SHUT to anything but PLAUSIBILITIES, common sense.

[SEE] = KNOW;

[HEAR] = TRUST the PERSON OF JESUS = FAITH.

Thomas DOESN'T BELIEVE YET.

Reason for this Gospel on 2 Easter.

Thomas, again. Second mention of CLOSED DOORS (Disciples' UNBELIEF, ἀπιστίαν, after 1st Easter). Our closed doors don't matter to Jesus: whether or not we BELIEVE it, he COMES IN to us, IS IN US — NOW!

22 καὶ τοῦτο εἰπὼν ἐνεφύσησεν καὶ λέγει αὐτοῖς, Λάβετε πνεῦμα ἅγιον· 23 ἄν τινων ἀφῆτε τὰς ἁμαρτίας ἀφέωνται αὐτοῖς, ἄν τινων κρατῆτε κεκράτηνται.

24 Θωμᾶς δὲ εἷς ἐκ τῶν δώδεκα, ὁ λεγόμενος Δίδυμος, οὐκ ἦν μετ' αὐτῶν ὅτε ἦλθεν Ἰησοῦς. 25 ἔλεγον οὖν αὐτῷ οἱ ἄλλοι μαθηταί, Ἑωράκαμεν τὸν κύριον. ὁ δὲ εἶπεν αὐτοῖς, Ἐὰν μὴ ἴδω ἐν ταῖς χερσὶν αὐτοῦ τὸν τύπον τῶν ἥλων καὶ βάλω τὸν δάκτυλόν μου εἰς τὸν τύπον τῶν ἥλων καὶ βάλω μου τὴν χεῖρα εἰς τὴν πλευρὰν αὐτοῦ, οὐ μὴ πιστεύσω.

26 Καὶ μεθ' ἡμέρας ὀκτὼ πάλιν ἦσαν ἔσω οἱ μαθηταὶ αὐτοῦ καὶ Θωμᾶς μετ' αὐτῶν. ἔρχεται ὁ Ἰησοῦς τῶν θυρῶν κεκλεισμένων καὶ ἔστη εἰς τὸ μέσον καὶ εἶπεν, Εἰρήνη ὑμῖν.

Revelation 4:1: "A DOOR was opened in heaven, and the first VOICE I HEARD was like a trumpet TALKING [FAITH] with me and saying, COME UP HERE and I will show you things that must be after this." THE [COSMIC OPEN DOOR] OF JESUS.

114

Jesus has presented HIMSELF as the SIGN OF FAITH. [THE SIGN OF JONAH] [THE STONE AT THE DOOR OF THE TOMB].

[FAITH WITHOUT KNOWING]. Jesus' SIGNS are not MIRACLES to astound the MIND but SACRAMENTS to elicit FAITH. John's passages about SIGNS all end with FAITH (πιστ). CANA, WOMAN AT WELL, BLIND MAN, THIS GOSPEL. Faith as OPINION vs. FAITH AS TRUST.

THE PURPOSE OF FAITH IS TO [HAVE A LIFE].

27 εἶτα λέγει τῷ Θωμᾷ, Φέρε τὸν δάκτυλόν σου ὧδε καὶ ἴδε τὰς χεῖράς μου, καὶ φέρε τὴν χεῖρά σου καὶ βάλε εἰς τὴν πλευράν μου, καὶ μὴ γίνου ἄπιστος ἀλλὰ πιστός.

28 ἀπεκρίθη Θωμᾶς καὶ εἶπεν αὐτῷ, Ὁ κύριός μου καὶ ὁ θεός μου. 29 λέγει αὐτῷ ὁ Ἰησοῦς, Ὅτι ἑώρακάς με πεπίστευκας; μακάριοι οἱ μὴ ἰδόντες καὶ πιστεύσαντες. 30 Πολλὰ μὲν οὖν καὶ ἄλλα σημεῖα ἐποίησεν ὁ Ἰησοῦς ἐνώπιον τῶν μαθητῶν [αὐτοῦ], ἃ οὐκ ἔστιν γεγραμμένα ἐν τῷ βιβλίῳ τούτῳ· 31 ταῦτα δὲ γέγραπται ἵνα πιστεύ[σ]ητε ὅτι Ἰησοῦς ἐστιν ὁ Χριστὸς ὁ υἱὸς τοῦ θεοῦ, καὶ ἵνα πιστεύοντες ζωὴν ἔχητε ἐν τῷ ὀνόματι αὐτου.

THEREFORE: " ... in order that BELIEVING, you might HAVE LIFE IN HIS NAME (PERSON). HAVE A LIFE, not GET A LIFE: IT'S A GIFT! IT'S FREE! IT'S YOURS, NOW! [GET A COOKIE! vs. HAVE A COOKIE!] — meaning, YOU OWN IT NOW! TAKE IT! ACCEPT IT! THAT'S THE [PEACE OF THE FINAL SUPPER — PARTY. WEDDING RECEPTION — OF THE LAMB] REVELA-TION 3:20: "I stand at the DOOR". *Pax tranquillitas ordinis* = PEACE IN THE HILARITY OF THAT PARTY.   *In Nomine Patris, etc.*

115

Sermon on the Gospel for the Second Sunday of Easter
(John 20:19-31, NRSV)

The Holy Gospel of our Lord Jesus Christ according to John

John 20:19 When it was evening on that day, the first day of the week, and the doors of the house where the disciples had met were locked for fear of the Jews, Jesus came and stood among them and said, "Peace be with you." 20 After he said this, he showed them his hands and his side. Then the disciples rejoiced when they saw the Lord. 21 Jesus said to them again, "Peace be with you. As the Father has sent me, so I send you." 22 When he had said this, he breathed on them and said to them, "Receive the Holy Spirit. 23 If you forgive the sins of any, they are forgiven them; if you retain the sins of any, they are retained." 24 But Thomas (who was called the Twin), one of the twelve, was not with them when Jesus came. 25 So the other disciples told him, "We have seen the Lord." But he said to them, "Unless I see the mark of the nails in his hands, and put my finger in the mark of the nails and my hand in his side, I will not believe." 26 A week later his disciples were again in the house, and Thomas was with them. Although the doors were shut, Jesus came and stood among them and said, "Peace be with you." 27 Then he said to Thomas, "Put your finger here and see my hands. Reach out your hand and put it in my side. Do not doubt but believe." 28 Thomas answered him, "My Lord and my God!" 29 Jesus said to him, "Have you believed because you have seen me? Blessed are those who have not seen and yet have come to believe." 30 Now Jesus did many other signs in the presence of his disciples, which are not written in this book. 31 But these are written so that you may come to believe that Jesus is the Messiah, the Son of God, and that through believing you may have life in his name. *The Gospel of the Lord.*

In the Name of the Father, and of the Son, and of the Holy Spirit. Amen.

Last Monday, when I took my first crack at trying to get a sermon out of today's Gospel, I noticed something odd about the passage. Jesus makes *two* resurrection appearances to the disciples in this story: one on the evening of Easter Day itself, when doubting Thomas wasn't present; and the other eight days later, when he was. And that, Virginia — since today is also the eighth day after Easter — is why the church reads this particular Gospel on this particular Sunday.

But there was more to it than that. Both of those appearances were strange — in fact, they were *weird.* John tells us that on each occasion, the doors where the disciples were staying were locked for fear of the Jews. But if you listened to the Gospel carefully, you realize that when Jesus does appear in the room, he gets there . . . well, he gets there simply by *showing up.* He doesn't knock. Nobody lets him in. He doesn't burst through the door in a flash of light, nor does he ooze his way through it like some special effect from a horror movie. Suddenly, he's just *inside,* without paying any attention to the door — as he was just *outside* at the tomb, without waiting for the stone to be rolled away. All he does is say, "Peace be with you"; then he stands there without a word and shows them his hands and his side — and "the disciples rejoiced when they saw the Lord." But how he got in there without anything happening (without a scrap of miraculous hocus-pocus), they never ask, and he never says.

Anyway, I started playing with those oddities; and between the locked doors of the disciples, and the notion of doors as such, and the alarmingly un-miraculous way Jesus got into the room, some ideas for this sermon began to percolate. So I did a search through the New Testament for all the references to "door," and it suddenly dawned on me that in addition to the two appearances of Jesus, there were also two kinds of doors here. What you see first, of course, are the disciples' doors — which can stand for all the locked doors of our lives: the doors that either trap us inside what we fear or outside what we want. But the second thing you see is Jesus himself as the Door: the Door who has installed himself

in every room of the world, and in every person in the world —
and who is open forever, no matter what else is locked. And there
was my theme: *our* doors versus *him as the Door*.

So I thought for a bit about the doors of our lives. Those are
the barricades we spend all our days on one side of or the other —
usually getting nowhere. They're the locked doors to health, wealth,
and happiness (the keys to which are almost always in somebody
else's pocket). They're the jammed gates to the pastures of
marriage, children, and career (the grass of which is always greener
on the other side of the fence). Still, we don't give up. In order to
get ourselves the life that lies on the other side of those doors, we
go at them with every religious key and psychological lockpick we
can find. But none of them opens easily, most don't open at all,
and all of them have a nasty tendency to close on our fingers.

Yet even as we stand knocking to be let in, there is always
Jesus, who (in the tenth chapter of John) says, "I am the door."
And he goes on to say, "I am the door of the sheep. Those who
enter through me will be saved and will go in and out and find
pasture." Do you see what that means? He isn't saying that he'll
come and lead us into the lush life we think is hiding on the other
side of the door we happen to be banging on. He's saying that *he*
is the Door. He's saying that our lifelong struggle to barge our way
in to better things for better living is *over*, because *in him* we've
already been led into life, and life abundant.

But at the end of my search, I came to the book of Revelation.
And there, in chapter three, was the glorified Jesus. In chapter one,
he stood in the midst of seven golden lampstands with a golden
sash across his chest, and he had eyes like a flame of fire and a
voice like the sound of many waters. And in chapter three, there
was that same Jesus, standing right before my eyes and saying,
"Behold, I stand at the door and knock; if you hear my voice and
open to me, I will come into your house, and I will eat with you,
and you will eat with me" (v. 20). You have to pardon the way my
mind works, but to me, this was nothing less than Jesus, the eternal
Party Animal, standing at my door (and yours) with the best take-

out food in the universe. This was the Supper of the Lamb, *brought home.*

Go back now and think a little more about those closed doors of ours. Before our birth, we spend nine months locked in the cubicle of our mother's womb, and it's the devil's own work for us to get out. Once out, though, things seem better. The door of infancy opens slowly into childhood, and the door of childhood eventually opens into adolescence. Yet at the same time, doors start to close as well as open. Our parents confront us with the door of No! Our schoolyard friends slam the door of You Can't Play! in our faces. And even less kind advisers introduce us to the most jammed door of all — the door of No Way!: "You just haven't got the ability to be a doctor; your SAT scores are too low. You'd be happier if you learned a trade."

We open the door of hope in our marriages, but all we ever find on the other side is someone who's as much in the dark as we are. We knock on the door of opportunity in our jobs, only to discover that getting the job was the last opportunity that presented itself. We lunge at the door of health armed with tofu, wheat germ, and canola oil; but we end up arthritic, doddering, or bald. We try to deal with the guilt-spattered doors of our sins by hosing them down with pure thoughts, religion, and psychiatry; yet we remain trapped behind them by our own history. But in the final analysis — having bravely attempted every door and boldly assaulted every doorkeeper — we come, abruptly and without being consulted, to the last door of all. We come to the one door that no mortal but Jesus has ever gotten past: we end up *dead.*

Which brings us back, nicely, to Jesus himself as the Door. Note well once again: he *is* the door; he doesn't just *do* doors. In spite of the fact that too many preachers (and most TV evangelists) tell us that if we pester Jesus enough, he'll help us break through to triumphant living — and make us thrifty, brave, clean, and reverent in the bargain — he just *won't.* He won't even promise to make us happy — at least not according to our recipe. But do you know why he won't? He won't because he has bigger fish to fry than the smelts of success we want him to cook for us. He's not interested in opening the doors of our choosing, because every now and then we might batter our way through one — and promptly pat ourselves on the back for being hotshot door openers. He isn't about to hand us a program for prying our way into our pet projects, because if he did that, most of us would fail the final exam, and the few of us who passed would be insufferable.

But Jesus doesn't want *most* or *some* or a *few*; his pet project is getting *all*. "I, if I be lifted up from the earth," he says in John 12:32 (and he means lifted up in his death) — "I, if I be lifted up from the earth, will draw *all* to myself." But since death is the only door in the world at which he can find the entire human race standing flat-footed and with nowhere to go — and since it's the door at which every last one of us will be deposited, seedy and by ourselves, without keys to open the lock, without strength to turn the handle, and with no wits left to think of a better place to be — it's in *death*, and death alone, that he chooses to offer himself as the Door of life. Only in death does he promise to do a blessed thing for us. Only where we least want to go will he make us what we most need to be.

Admittedly, he did open a few doors for a handful of the blind, lame, and sick. And he raised three dead bodies, staged two spectacular mass feedings, and once produced 180 gallons of wine for a wedding reception whose guests were already three sheets to the wind. But he was stingy with those miraculous interventions — and he apparently had no intention whatsoever of poking them into the lives of everybody and his sister. Those grand openings of closed doors were not his program; they were simply the signs of it. His program was to break down the door of death by getting locked behind it himself — and then to escape scot-free in his resurrection.

Do you now see why he did it that way? He chose the certainty of death over our undependable efforts to "get a life" because he apparently found it the only way he could draw all instead of some. *Jesus came to raise the dead,* not to improve the improvable, not to cure the curable, not to teach the teachable. Any such program would have netted him about two dozen fish out of the entire ocean of human history. Eternal life and everlasting happiness would have been for the handful of over-achievers who could save their own lives. The great, gray-green, greasy mass of humanity would still be out there drowning in the drink.

It is in his death, therefore — by the motionless drawing of his Love and the silent voice of his Calling — that he becomes the Door of life for everybody. For Christian, Jew, and Buddhist; for the believer and the non-believer; for the saints and the scoundrels — and for all of us grandly average souls who are not so good and not so bad, but very definitely indifferent. But by our great good luck in the dead and risen Lord, that makes the only ticket any of us needs the one ticket all of us have. We're all dead, and our life is hid with Christ in God. We don't have to go tearing around trying to make contact with Jesus in order to get him to be Life for us. He's the Door of life for us right now, because he's in our death right now. Our death is the largest fact of our life. My last gasp will be my biggest guarantee that I'll draw the breath of life forever.

Still, Jesus doesn't just stand and knock at the door of my deathbed; he stands at the doors of all my "deaths before death," great and small. If the catastrophes of my history are his cup of tea, the minor scrapes and bruises of my life are his biscuits. The old tempter, Screwtape, told his underling, Wormwood, that when it comes to getting someone into hell, "murder is no better than cards, if cards will do the trick." Jesus says that for bringing me to heaven, my color blindness is no less useful to him as a "death" than my total blindness would be. As far as he's concerned, even a hangnail is enough of a death for him to grant me resurrection.

So there's not a single door of mine that's too small for his attention — and, best of all, any death he finds me in will be where he does his best work. Even if I ignore him, he'll go right on doing it. His gift of life in death doesn't depend on my listening for his knock and then running to the door to let him in. He comes into the house of my death without my help. I can decide not to listen to him at all — and I can do nothing whatsoever about opening myself to him — but he'll be as much there in the room of my death as he is in the room where we see the disciples gathered today.

"The hour is coming and now is," Jesus says, "when the dead will hear the voice of the Son of God, and they that hear will live." He doesn't mean the cooperative dead, or the morally upright dead, or the spiritually proficient dead. He means the dead dead — the plain, buried, gone corpses who are all his voice needs to make a new creation. And when he says, "they that hear will live," he doesn't mean those who "listen to" or "obey" or "agree with" that voice. The dead are beyond all that — and besides, Jesus has no use for any of it. He simply means that his voice has such a bark to it that the dead come stark-staring upright at the sound, no matter what. He means that his knock has such force that it flattens all the doors in its way. He means that his voice and his knock are present to us now — not just at the last day of our lives, or the Last Day of the universe. As Jesus in this Gospel was there inside his disciples' locked doors, so today he is here inside yours. I want to read you something that John Donne, the Dean of St.Paul's Cathedral in London, said in a sermon he preached on Christmas Day in the Evening, 1624:

> *To day* if you will heare his voice, *to day* he will heare you. . . .
> Though in the wayes of fortune, or understanding, or conscience,
> thou have been benighted till now, wintred and frozen, clouded
> and eclypsed, damped and benummbed, smothered and stupefied
> till now, now God comes to thee, not as in the dawning of the
> day, not as in the bud of spring, but as the Sun at noon to illustrate
> all shadowes, as the sheaves in harvest, to fill all penuries, all
> occasions invite his mercies, and all times are his seasons.

Now that's preaching!

Which brings us to part two of the theme of this sermon: some reflections on the *second* appearance of the risen Jesus in our Gospel — the appearance for which Thomas was present.

Thomas's problem is that his mind is shut. He's locked behind the door of thinking he can't trust Jesus to be risen unless he can prove it for himself — unless he can know it rather than believe it. So when Jesus appears this time to the disciples, he devotes almost his entire visit to the subject of *faith*. After he gives them all his "Peace be with you" greeting again, he ignores the rest and goes straight to Thomas.

"Okay, Thomas," he says; "I'll go along with your doubts for a minute — but only for a minute. Put your finger here and look at my hand, and reach out your hand and put it in my side. Then stop all this doubting and believe." And Thomas says, "My Lord and my God!" You pay your money and take your choice here. Maybe those words meant that Thomas was breaking through to faith. Maybe, though, they just meant something like "Wow!" Since I lean toward the latter interpretation, let me explain.

In the Bible, seeing often does duty for knowing. Jesus said, "Unless you see signs and wonders [he means "as long as you think you have to glom on to something you can know"], there's no way you're going to believe." But that truth prevails outside the Bible as well. Even in ordinary life, we use the same analogy. When somebody says, I "see," she means "I understand, I know, I've got it." Take my own case right now. I don't *believe* that you people are sitting out there in those pews; I *know* you're there because I see you right in front of me.

But when I don't see something, I can do nothing but believe it. Suppose that Harry, our sterling organist over there, stands up right now and says, "Robert, I'll give you ten thousand dollars if you'll just shut up and sit down." If that happens, I have a problem that can't be solved by knowing. My problem is not that I am unsure about Harry's motives: I know nothing about them. Nor is my problem that shutting up will look like a betrayal of my calling for thirty pieces of silver. I'm as free as the wind to take his money, and, since he said nothing about my shutting up next Sunday, to preach the rest of my sermon then.

My real problem is that I don't know anything that will help me make a decision about whether or not to take Harry up on his offer. He hasn't flashed his money in front of me. He hasn't volunteered to let me examine his bank statements. For all I know, he hasn't got a dime to his name. All that my mind can do with his promise to give me a bundle for my silence is doubt it — like Thomas. I can understand what he's promising me, but for me to get the benefit of his ten big ones, I'm going to have to *trust* him to be as good as his word. So, as *seeing* does duty for *knowing, hearing* is the stand-in for *faith*. Even if Harry's got the money he's told me he's willing to part with, I'll go right on being as broke as I am if I don't *believe* him.

Still, I've got to do more than "believe" in the sense of "have an opinion" about him, or "think" that he'll pay me. It doesn't matter squat what I think or opine. If Harry's set on getting out his checkbook, he'll do it. If not, not. But even supposing he is, and I don't *trust* him — if I get up on my intellectual high horse and insist on waiting for proof to come along — I'll never come within a million miles of his bonanza.

I've led you through that "seeing-slash-knowing, hearing-slash-believing" detour for a reason. I took you there because Jesus' next words to Thomas aren't flattering. He doesn't say, "Oh, good for you, Thomas, for getting around to deciding I'm your Lord and God. You're my beamish boy!" He goes right for the jugular and says, "So, Thomas; you think you've believed because you've seen, eh? Well, I'll tell you something: the happy people are those who *don't* see, because they're the only ones who can believe."

That may or may not be a fair reading of Jesus' words. He's not always easy to figure out. But it's a cinch to figure out why the evangelist put these particular words here. In today's lesson, we're in the twentieth chapter of the Gospel according to John (there are only twenty-one chapters in the book); therefore, he's beginning to wrap up everything he's said about Jesus. And since John's sole purpose in writing was to lead his readers to faith in Jesus, believing has got to be the finale of his finale. Many times before now, he's tipped his hand to the necessity of faith. In every account he's given of one of Jesus' signs (that's the word he uses: the plain old Greek for "sign," not fancy, spiritual words like "miracle" or "mighty act" or "frightening deed"), he ends his narration not with the oohs and aahs of the miracle mongers but with the announcement that somebody believed in Jesus.

And here, at the end of today's Gospel, he's up to the same trick. He elbows Jesus aside and takes over the narrative himself. What follows in the rest of this passage is *John* talking, not Jesus: in his best wrap-up style, he says, "Therefore: Jesus did many other signs in his disciples' presence, and I've by no means written all of them down in this book. But *these signs* happened in order that you might *believe* that Jesus is the Son of God — and that *believing*, you might have life in his name."

The reason for having faith is not to get a life. It's to have, to hold, and to embrace the life that Jesus (who is our Way, and our Truth, and our Life) has already given us by his presence in our death. Our faith is blind trust in a Person, not clear-sighted confidence in some scheme that God has concocted to help us feel good about ourselves. It's our mere acquiescence to a gift we already have in Jesus, not a negotiation by which we try to wangle it out of him. God's whole gift of acceptance in his Beloved Son is ours now. We own it, for Christ's sake! We ought at least to have the manners to enjoy it.

Let me close with an illustration that takes off from the picture of Jesus the Party Bringer who was standing at our door in the passage from Revelation I quoted at the beginning of this sermon. Imagine him with me. He has in his hand a giant tray of goodies that he's bought at The Barefoot Contessa, or Zabar's, or any place you'd like to name — as long as the food is outrageously expensive and fabulously good. So when he finally appears in your house, having made short work of all the locked doors of your life, make no mistake about what he'll say. He won't say, "What have you *got* for supper?" or "Why don't you *get* us something to drink?" He'll say, *"Have* some *foie gras! Have* a quail egg! *Have* the flourless, double-chocolate cake!" He'll say, *"Take, eat,"* not *"Fetch!"* He'll say, *have!*, not *get!* And he'll say *have!* because all his gifts are yours, *now*.

By his one oblation of himself once offered in his death as a full, perfect, and sufficient sacrifice, oblation, and satisfaction for all the doors you ever waited in front of with your hat in your hand — and by the great gifts of his Blessed Passion and Precious Death, his Mighty Resurrection and his Glorious Ascension — he will say that today he has heard your voice, and that today, and forever, you *own* them.

And therefore on all your days before this day, and on all your days after it — and on all days, for all creatures, from the foundation of the world to the end of time — they have always been yours. And they've been yours because he is your Lord and your God, and he brings you out of the nothing of your death as easily as he brought you out of the nothing before your birth. The Party that is Jesus is the party to end all parties. It's yours now, and it's on now. In the unending hilarity of that Party, you have been sprung forever into the liberty with which Christ has made you free — into the Peace that passes understanding. Just trust him, and enjoy it.

Calm down about your life, pour yourself a glass of the *Chateau Haut Brion* he's brought you, and kick back. Finally and for good, you're *Home!*

In the Name of the Father, and of the Son, and of the Holy Spirit. Amen.

*   *   *

Now then. Let's have our chat.

I have no idea whether you liked that sermon or not. In either case, I'll say "Good!" and let it go at that. As you know, I haven't preached regularly from a manuscript since the first months of my ministry — although I've given written-out sermons on a few "state occasions," such as ordinations. Still, since I'm reasonably happy with my results in this instance, I'll tell you why.

First, my time sheet for the work I put in on it. It took a good

many more hours than the eight I put in on the "notes" version.
Today is the Friday of the week in which I began this chapter. I
spent last Monday cleaning up the notes for 2 Easter and getting
the previous week's unfinished business off my desk. I spent
Tuesday, Wednesday, and Thursday writing the sermon — at the
rate of eight, eight, and seven hours, respectively: 8 + 8 + 7 = 23
hours. That's not only respectable, it's heroic — and I can hear your
reaction to it. "My God! He may have resigned from the parish
treadmill, but I haven't. Does he seriously think I'm going to find
that kind of time?"

No, I don't. Forget that. I want to talk about the sermon itself.

As I see it, it has a good, long middle and a fairly hefty ending.
But that's pretty much it. If it has any beginning, it's nothing more
than the first sentence of the first paragraph. After that, the sermon
is all middle until you get to the last two paragraphs, where I turned
on the purple prose and ended in an attempt at the grand homiletical style. Still, don't let that encourage you to think lush language
alone can make a sermon end well. The three things you might
learn from what I did are to begin without an overblown warmup,
to head straight for the game itself — and to stay in it until you
spot a hole through which you can bolt to the end zone without
running off the sidelines of your subject.

Oh, right. I did purple things up a bit with John Donne near
the end of the first half. But then I went right back to my usual
style, which is a gallimaufry of exposition, teaching, analogies, and
shtick. If I have any style at all, it's that I do Bible, theology, high
homiletics, and low comedy all at once. Nonetheless, I'm even
farther from suggesting you copy me in that than I was from
suggesting you put in hours like mine. The only person you can
hope to emulate is yourself; your style must flow out of your own
interests and talents, not out of somebody else's. No matter how
much you may admire another preacher's gift of gab, that way lies
the madness of standing up in clothes that don't fit and preaching
in a language you'll never master. Don't *imitate!*

You might, however (without imitating any particular thing I did in that sermon), borrow a page from the way I wrote it. At as many points as possible, I tried to make it a smorgasbord of contrasting flavors. It was meant to be inviting, funny, flirtatious (even seductive) — and, as I said, conversational. To be honest, it took me four or five passes through the manuscript to sweep away the tired onion skins and potato peelings I'd left lying around on the computer cutting-board and make room for fresher phrases.

One note. If my illustrations come largely from the food business, that's because it's one of the businesses I happen to be crazy about. But the lesson there is that when you preach, you have a better chance of sounding as if you're talking *to* people rather than *at* them if you illustrate your sermons with images drawn from subjects you delight in and know something about. Football, bird-watching, tennis, or golf; woodworking, stamp-collecting, or jogging; real estate, banking, or taking naps: all of those can be delicious, provided you're nuts enough about them to sound like an *insider* talking.

(One other note. The previous sentence embodies one of the cardinal principles of public speaking: always use concrete illustrations. Don't say, "Sports, hobbies, and business experiences are acceptable illustrations": open up those closed portmanteaus. Show pictures to your listeners. Oh! — and one more: Don't be afraid of slang: it's the salt of speaking. Too much of it, of course, will make your style off-putting; but just enough makes your sermon sound as if you mean it.)

As you can see, there's no great order to this conversation we're having; we're just going with the flow. The next thing that's coming down the stream is something that occurred to me in the midst of those last few don'ts. Writing a sermon is not an exercise in scholarship. A scholarly book is often a dreadful book because the sequence of the argument — the clothesline on which the author hangs up the soggy wash of her notes — has nothing but the left-brained logic of the last order into which she shuffled her index cards.

In a sermon, though, as in any good conversation, what comes next has to come out of your reaction to what you just heard yourself say, and out of your sense of your hearers' reactions to it. A natural-sounding order will always conform to the "logic of the imagination" that's the specialty of the right side of the brain. That's why it's important to *talk* your sermon into being. If you write with a pad and pencil, you have to hear what you're saying, not just look at it. If you compose on the computer, it's even more important. You have to keep up a constant conversation with the screen — preferably out loud (at least that will keep you from smoking too much) — until the finished-looking banalities in front of you sound like you. That's the only kind of talk the folks out in front will bother listening to. So freely dis-associate yourself from the crud and mumble at the machine until it's not cruddy anymore. (This becomes especially important the closer you get to your final edit: if you don't do it, you'll come off sounding like three other people, all of whom are bores.)

In short, learn to trust your talking mind and your listening ear. Trust your innate sense (I hope you have one) of sequence. Trust your alertness to passages that are too tight — that are concentrated orange juice and need dilution with explanatory sentences if your congregation is to keep up with the all-too-sudden leaps of your left brain. Trust your sense of pacing. You can sometimes (with great effect) write sentences that have a hundred words in them — and get away with it, if you do it right. But if you don't precede or follow them with very short sentences, you might as well be reading IRS regulations. You must surround your sesquipedalian creations with terse sentences. Punchy sentences. Sentences without verbs. And in particular, sentences without adverbs.

Note that last one well. Don't write "really punchy sentences." Or "sentences entirely without adverbs." Adverbs and adjectives pull punches more often than they deliver them. On the other hand, don't be ruthless and yank them all. Conversations are loaded with them.

Likewise, don't be afraid of peppering your sermon text with *italics.* Since you'll have to read your sermon out loud and as convincingly as possible — since it's going to be an *oral* experience for you and an *aural* experience for your congregation — be as *generous* with them as you like in your manuscript. *Besides: italics* will spare you the embarrassment of stumbling over your own words as if you'd never heard them before. They'll help you not to sound like an idiot.

Above all, though, trust your God-given ear for windiness — and turn it on yourself with a vengeance. Delete! Delete! Delete! until your soporifics have been banished, and only crispness is left. A good many of the twenty-three hours I put in on the sermon I gave you were spent giving the heave-ho to my own tiresomeness. That's not so easy for an author to spot, you know. If you just look at a drone-on sentence you've written, you won't see what a dozer it is. You have to hear it. You have to inflict it on yourself by letting it come out of your mouth and into your ear. Because unless you're a lot better than most preachers, you're infected with the notion that respectable writing calls for a voice that's serious to the point of stuffiness. Learn what your normal, conversational voice sounds like; and then *gnaw* on the bones of your sentences until you've stripped them down to nothing but that sound.

An example, drawn right from the preceding paragraph: My first attempt at the last sentence was "Learn what your ordinary, talking voice sounds like, and then ruthlessly take out everything that doesn't match that sound." But since almost anybody can ruthlessly take or leave anything on earth, I preliminarily got rid of it in favor of "hack" — which was more aggressive, and a four-letter word to boot. Then I wrote, "Learn what your ordinary, talking voice sounds like, and *hack away* at your sentences till they match it." After that, I got an even better idea: I got a mental image of a lion gnawing at a carcass, so I'll work that in right here. Here goes the rest of this paragraph: "Sit every word in your sermon down in the dentist's chair and do a root canal on it. You don't want adjectives and adverbs with dentures; you want nouns and verbs with teeth. Those are parts of speech that can make you sound like someone who's not to be messed with. Why should you come across like a pussycat when you can have the molars of a lion?''

The hit-or-miss logic of this gabfest now reminds me of what I consider the single, best writing trick I ever learned: When you write, never interrupt yourself (unless the house is on fire) at the end of a paragraph, section, or chapter. Always take your break in the middle of something. I'll give you an instance. In the middle of that last paragraph (where I'd written ". . . image of a lion gnawing at a carcass''), I paused to refill my pipe. I stopped there just as I was about to write, "Why should you sound worse (or even *dumber*) than you are?" But when I heard that in my mind, it seemed derogatory, and I wanted to change it. So after I lit up and went back to work, the pussycat/lion gambit popped into my head. And then I went back to the paragraph before that and changed *hack* to *gnaw*.

I learned about this device of not stopping yourself at the end of a finished thought from Anthony Trollope's *Autobiography*. (I also learned from him to write early in the morning — though I never mastered his trick of writing with a watch next to him and producing a page every fifteen minutes. Ah, well. Trollope was Trollope; Capon isn't.) Anyway, the best thing about his "interruption rule" is that if you follow it every time you quit writing for the day — and just scribble in some key words about where you were going — you will come back the next day not to the nasty prospect of a blank space (and the dog-work of rummaging through your notes for something new — and thus harder to say), but to a thought in progress that you can pick up on as easily as if you'd never stopped writing. Try it. It may be the best piece of advice in this book.

I detect a cloud of fussiness passing over your mind. Having spotted the adverbial "as easily as" just now, you're about to charge me yet again with ignoring my own advice. *Nolo contendere*. I do use adverbs rather freely. I even use clichés with gay abandon. So if you insist on a guilty plea, I'll enter one — but with an explanation: That's the way I talk, so I frequently let it stand. Especially if it sounds a little trite. Lends a common touch and all that.

Which brings up the matter of vocabulary that's lurking somewhere in your cloud. Don't be leery of words and phrases like "crud" and "great stuff." Preachers who avoid "crud" because it doesn't sound dignified (or, God help us, homiletical) are missing out on the chance to express their dislike of nonsense in one trenchant word, rather than stuff it into an oversize suitcase like "distasteful inanity" or "tiresome verbosity." And preachers who use "impressive material" to avoid "great stuff" are peddling Sleep-Eeze when they ought to be selling No-Dōz.

Still, you have to be careful about colloquialisms. All through this book I've been dying to do a riff on the spelling of the River Styx that Greek mythology put between this world and Hades: once you'd been ferried across it by grisly old Charon, you could never get back. My idea was to make a pun on "Styx." I very nearly put it in my sermon — back there when I was saying that Jesus "just *won't*" help you get out of your troubles and take you back to the dandy life you think you deserve. I wanted to say something like, ". . . he just *won't*. He never promised to deliver us from the Hades of our lives by ferrying us back across the river of Shyt that surrounds us and taking us "back" to the land of health, money, and love. Bizarrely, he tells us that he's jumped into the Shyt with us and drowned in it. And then he invites us to believe that he's drained the damned stream once and for all in his resurrection." But on second thought, I didn't do that. Not because it was inappropriate — and certainly not because there were any chaste ears out there that would be terminally offended by it. I left it unsaid because the pun on "Styx" that made "Shyt" funny to the eye would be lost on a congregation who could only hear it with their ears.

Having hit the *italics* keys in this chapter more times than Tylenol has capsules, it suddenly occurs to me that almost everything in this book is a demonstration of the *conversational* style of preaching. At the price of avoiding elegance and correctness, I've given you a running lesson in writing the way human beings talk. I know. I wander. But since I can't tell you everything about writing, I'm telling you anything that strikes my fancy. I press on.

A few more random don'ts and we're done. First, don't *ever* hand your sermon to someone else to type. Unless you're a genius whose second draft never needs revising, that's a snare: your sermon is going to come back from your secretary's labors of love looking so neat and clean that you'll believe your work on it is done. If you type it yourself, you'll know what a mess it is — and you'll probably do a halfway decent job of tidying it up. You don't type well, you say? That's no excuse. You couldn't possibly be a worse typist than I am. Just do it! Yourself!

Next, don't spend any time worrying about your critics, real or imagined. Don't pander to them; annoy them, rattle their cages. You're supposed to be a rotten little kid, remember? Stop trying to come across to them, as the French (ah, those French!) say, "like an infant Jesus in velvet pants." Most of your people haven't a clue as to what you're supposed to be up to in the pulpit — and the few who might have an inkling of what you were ordained to do still have no idea what it's like to produce a sermon every seven days for at least forty-eight weeks a year. All that should matter to you is that *you* have a clue. And a lot more than a clue: a *conviction*.

Nobody says stuff like this anymore, but I'm going to say what that conviction is. As their ordained preacher, you must know in your bones that you're in a position of *authority* over them. I'll soften that a little by calling it a position of *authenticity* for them; but I refuse to boil it down any further, lest it get limp. You're not just a nice Alex up there entertaining them with routines they want to hear. If you give in to them and preach jolly anecdotes, old jokes, and ethical bromides, they'll smile at you — mostly, I think, because they know they've won you over. On the other hand, if you preach them the weird Good News of the God incarnate who makes the wrecks of their lives his favorite workshop, they'll frown — and give you all the hassles they can dish out. They don't like being bitten by the Gospel. They'd rather be gummed to death by platitudes.

So don't give them a scrap of power over you; don't trim your sails to the shifting winds of their unparadoxical minds. On certain days, they'll berate you for preaching the universal grace of Jesus because they know perfectly well that it condemns them to an eternity with the millions they won't forgive. On others, they'll decide that God's indiscriminate acceptance of everybody in the Beloved — by the outrageous stunt of being present in every death, no matter how disreputable — is an affront to truth, justice, and the American Way. But on all days, they'll think that they're right and you're wrong.

You must always be patient with them, of course. They've sat too long under preachers who catered to their enthusiasm for uplift by their own bootstraps — and you're probably the first one who ever tried to take away that security blanket. In the long run, though, what you must say to them is what Luther said at the Diet of Worms: *"Hie steh' ich; ich kann nichts anders"*:"Here I stand; I can do no other." You must make them know that you're under authority in the pulpit — and that you're nothing less than the voice of that authority. You were not sent to spout opinions they can dismiss. You were sent to proclaim the sharp, authentic Word to them — the Word who isn't NutraSweet. Tell them that no preacher worth his or her salt ever turned the Gospel into a trade-marked substitute for the authentic sweetness of Jesus' death — and that you're not about to risk it yourself.

This becomes crucial if you've got a "Pulpit Committee" breathing down your neck. The favorite tack of such busybodies is to inform you that many (always unnamed) parishioners are upset by your sermons. Cut off their wind. Sail right up next to them and stop them dead with the retort I always give to such types (it will help if it's true of you, too): "I don't gossip, and I never listen to gossips. If people give you a complaint about my preaching, tell them to make an appointment and get it off their chest with me in person. That way, maybe they and I can be responsible enough to get somewhere with it. This way, we're just playing chin music. Thank you, and good night!"

The pulpit is no place for Milquetoasts. You must not allow your authenticity to be questioned. Arrogance for Christ's sake is not the first thing to be avoided. What you most need to be on guard against is your longing to be seen as a humble servant and a good egg. Your people may charge you with arrogance; but that's because they think your authoritative ways are a front for your fear of being made a doormat — which, incidentally, is probably the use they have in mind for you. Sass them back: as the man said, "It ain't braggin' if I can do it." Tell them you're perfectly happy to be a doormat — but that you insist on being a real one. They think you imagine yourself as a Persian rug, and that you're terrified at the prospect of even a single muddy footprint. Let them find out that you're a plain old sisal mat who can get rid of all the dirt they wipe on you with two good shakes. And give them no choice but to believe you because you believe it from the soles of your feet. Dogs and pulpit committees can smell fear — and both go snarling after anyone who runs scared. In the name of the Gospel, you've got to be the stronger dog.

But that, I think, will do it. One more chapter that lies halfway between the subject of preaching from notes and that of preaching from a manuscript, and we'll be ready for the wrap-up.

ELEVEN

Synchronicity, Serendipity, Spontaneity

No system of sermon preparation works all the time. In this book, I've spelled out mine for you — sometimes as if I'd been laying down the law from Mount Sinai. But by now, you know me better. I sit loose to my own commandments, and I have no illusions of your following them slavishly. Nevertheless, there's one regulation that's served me so well I want to give you a brief example to underscore it.

That's the one about having your notes in preachable shape no later than Saturday morning. I urged that on you because I wanted you to be free first thing on Sunday morning to devote all your attention to the preaching of them, not to diddling them into niftier shape. What I want to do now is urge you to remain open, even at that final hour of preparation, to the possibility of radically revising your sermon. This is Monday of the week of 4 Easter. What I'm about to tell you happened between four and ten A.M. yesterday.

When I got ready for bed on Saturday night, I made a note on the scratch pad I keep around for sudden illuminations. It read, "Remember: the best ideas may occur to you on Sunday early — when you're finally ready to grapple with the prospect of preaching as opposed to just thinking about it. Your adrenaline is beginning to flow: go with it. You're on! Don't screw around with your notes on the computer. Don't try to keep your notes pristine. Just scribble all over the damned things. Change them radically if you have to. Stick Post-its here, there, and everywhere. Only now, perhaps, after your preparation is behind you, will you see where your sermon is actually supposed to go and what it's really about." (That message was written with you in mind, but it turned out to be for me — with a vengeance.)

As I hit the sack, though, a thought passed through my mind. My sermon for the next day struck me as . . . well, bland, impersonal. Something upsetting had occurred in our household two days before, and it seemed chicken of me to get up in the pulpit and prattle away as if it hadn't happened. That was as far as I went before I drifted off to sleep. But in the morning, just as I was getting out of bed, a radical revision came to me in a flash: I'd narrate the story of what happened, and then expound the two lessons I'd chosen to preach on in the light of it, and vice versa. And so I did. An hour-and-a-half of making a mess of my notes, and I had a sermon instead of a snorer. Best of all, it was not going to be the kind of thing I usually preach.

What follows is the paper trail of that transformation. First, I'll give you my notes on the 4 Easter propers as I had them before me when I sat down at 4:00 on Sunday morning. I won't clean them up or give you any comments on them; they'll just lie before you now as they lay before me then: a sermon that wasn't going to be preached. Next, I won't burden you with what's missing from the trail, namely, the unreadable, hen-scratched, hard copy I preached from — and the many drafts I produced at the computer as I pulled and hauled to get those notes into intelligible (?) shape. Just trust me: I produced a lot of scrap paper. Finally, then, I'll give you the notes as I've now considerably expanded them in order to show you how I actually preached the sermon. Then a quick bridge to the Epilogue, and we're outta here.

Here are the lessons I preached on:

RSV 1 Peter 2:19 For one is approved if, mindful of God, he endures pain while suffering unjustly. 20 For what credit is it, if when you do wrong and are beaten for it you take it patiently? But if when you do right and suffer for it you take it patiently, you have God's approval. 21 For to this you have been called, because Christ also suffered for you, leaving you an example, that you should follow in his steps. 22 He committed no sin; no guile was found on his lips. 23 When he was reviled, he did not revile in return; when he suffered, he did not threaten; but he trusted to him who judges justly. 24 He himself bore our sins in his body on the tree, that we might die to sin and live to righteousness. By his wounds you have been healed. 25 For you were straying like sheep, but have now returned to the Shepherd and Guardian of your souls.

RSV John 10:1 "Truly, truly, I say to you, he who does not enter the sheepfold by the door but climbs in by another way, that man is a thief and a robber; 2 but he who enters by the door is the shepherd of the sheep. 3 To him the gatekeeper opens; the sheep hear his voice, and he calls his own sheep by name and leads them out. 4 When he has brought out all his own, he goes before them, and the sheep follow him, for they know his voice. 5 A stranger they will not follow, but they will flee from him, for they do not know the voice of strangers." 6 This figure Jesus used with them, but they did not understand what he was saying to them. 7 So Jesus again said to them, "Truly, truly, I say to you, I am the door of the sheep. 8 All who came before me are thieves and robbers; but the sheep did not heed them. 9 I am the door; if any one enters by me, he will be saved, and will go in and out and find pasture. 10 The thief comes only to steal and kill and destroy; I came that they may have life, and have it abundantly."

In Nomine Patris, etc. In the READING from 1 Peter and in the GOSPEL, we have the IMAGES of SHEPHERD, SHEEP, & DOOR and we have the subject of loss of CONTROL. I'm going to expound BOTH at the same time.

ON: ↓↓

Jesus HIMSELF is the [DOOR]."

Tries to ROB them by [ILLUSION of CONTROL]."

GNT John 10:1 Ἀμὴν ἀμὴν λέγω ὑμῖν, ὁ μὴ εἰσερχόμενος διὰ τῆς θύρας εἰς τὴν αὐλὴν τῶν προβάτων ἀλλὰ ἀναβαίνων ἀλλαχόθεν ἐκεῖνος κλέπτης ἐστὶν καὶ λῃστής·

"[RH/LH CONTROL] suffering because of LH control.

"SUFFERING because of RH :control.

"vs. PATIENCE under LH control.

"[GRACE] = Trust / Favor. Approval.

GNT 1 Peter 2:19 τοῦτο γὰρ χάρις εἰ διὰ συνείδησιν θεοῦ ὑποφέρει τις λύπας πάσχων ἀδίκως 20 ποῖον γὰρ κλέος εἰ ἁμαρτάνοντες καὶ κολαφιζόμενοι ὑπομενεῖτε; ἀλλ᾽ εἰ ἀγαθοποιοῦντες καὶ πάσχοντες ὑπομενεῖτε, τοῦτο χάρις παρὰ θεῷ.

SHEPHERD & BISHOP"

θυρωρὸς = CHURCH?!"

2 ὁ δὲ εἰσερχόμενος διὰ τῆς θύρας ποιμήν ἐστιν τῶν προβάτων 3 τούτῳ ὁ θυρωρὸς ἀνοίγει, καὶ τὰ πρόβατα τῆς φωνῆς αὐτοῦ ἀκούει καὶ τὰ ἴδια πρόβατα φωνεῖ κατ᾽ ὄνομα καὶ ἐξάγει αὐτά 4 ὅταν τὰ ἴδια πάντα ἐκβάλῃ,

"OUR CALLING is to follow him into his [LH POWER] in OUR disasters as in HIS.

21 εἰς τοῦτο γὰρ ἐκλήθητε, ὅτι καὶ Χριστὸς ἔπαθεν ὑπὲρ ὑμῶν ὑμῖν ὑπολιμπάνων ὑπογραμμὸν ἵνα ἐπακολουθήσητε τοῖς ἴχνεσιν αὐτοῦ,

22 ὃς ἁμαρτίαν οὐκ ἐποίησεν οὐδὲ εὑρέθη δόλος ἐν τῷ στόματι αὐτοῦ,

23 ὃς λοιδορούμενος οὐκ ἀντελοιδόρει, πάσχων οὐκ ἠπείλει, παρεδίδου δὲ τῷ κρίνοντι δικαίως· 24 ὃς τὰς ἁμαρτίας ἡμῶν αὐτὸς ἀνήνεγκεν ἐν τῷ σώματι αὐτοῦ ἐπὶ τὸ ξύλον, ἵνα ταῖς ἁμαρτίαις ἀπογενόμενοι τῇ δικαιοσύνῃ ζήσωμεν, οὗ τῷ μώλωπι ἰάθητε.

They FLEE at CONTROLLING advice.**

**HE ESCHEWS CONTROL!!!

**He meets our sins in his DEATH.
**We're FREE from OTHERS' SINS as well.
**HE is our PEACE!

ἔμπροσθεν αὐτῶν πορεύεται, καὶ τὰ πρόβατα αὐτῷ ἀκολουθεῖ, ὅτι οἴδασιν τὴν φωνὴν αὐτοῦ·

5 ἀλλοτρίῳ δὲ οὐ μὴ ἀκολουθήσουσιν, ἀλλὰ φεύξονται ἀπ' αὐτοῦ, ὅτι οὐκ οἴδασιν τῶν ἀλλοτρίων τὴν φωνήν.

6 Ταύτην τὴν παροιμίαν εἶπεν αὐτοῖς ὁ Ἰησοῦς, ἐκεῖνοι δὲ οὐκ ἔγνωσαν τίνα ἦν ἃ ἐλάλει αὐτοῖς. 7 Εἶπεν οὖν πάλιν ὁ Ἰησοῦς, Ἀμὴν ἀμὴν λέγω ὑμῖν ὅτι ἐγώ εἰμι ἡ θύρα τῶν προβάτων. 8 πάντες ὅσοι ἦλθον [πρὸ ἐμοῦ] κλέπται εἰσὶν καὶ λῃσταί, ἀλλ' οὐκ ἤκουσαν αὐτῶν τὰ πρόβατα.

PARABLE, COMPARISON
As usual, they miss the point.**

[DOOR AGAIN]**

CONTROLLING thieves & robbers, above.**
The sheep get nowhere under their ADVICE.**

140

25 ἦτε γὰρ ὡς πρόβατα πλανώμενοι, ἀλλὰ ἐπεστράφητε νῦν ἐπὶ τὸν ποιμένα καὶ ἐπίσκοπον τῶν ψυχῶν ὑμῶν

Only under the LH SHEPHERDING of Jesus are we SAFE!!!**

**SHEPHERD & BISHOP

Only Jesus' LH control can give us LIFE. **

9 ἐγώ εἰμι ἡ θύρα· δι' ἐμοῦ ἐάν τις εἰσέλθη σωθήσεται καὶ εἰσελεύσεται καὶ ἐξελεύσεται καὶ νομὴν εὑρήσει.

10 ὁ κλέπτης οὐκ ἔρχεται εἰ μὴ ἵνα κλέψη καὶ θύση καὶ ἀπολέση· ἐγὼ ἦλθον ἵνα ζωὴν ἔχωσιν καὶ περισσὸν ἔχωσιν.

THEREFORE: LIFE & LIFE ABUNDANT!!! TRUST HIM IN THE PARADOX OF FAITH!!! *In Nomine Patris etc.*

141

⊕ 4 Easter, Year A, 28apr96. R. F. Capon, *Sermon on Shepherd, Door, Control (1 Peter 2:19-25; John 10:1-10)*   Home   page 1

In Nomine Patris, etc. In the 2nd Reading (1 Peter) and in the Gospel (John 10), we have IMAGES of SHEPHERD, SHEEP, and DOOR. I'm going to expound BOTH lessons at the same time, tying them to our DREAD of LOSING CONTROL over our lives, and using a [PERSONAL ILLUSTRATION]:

NEAR COLLISION: It's 5:00 p.m. I'm driving on a 4-lane divided highway, taking Valerie and her 3 grandchildren to see my granddaughter play the lead in a 4th-grade production of *Cinderella*. (We're headed for MacDonald's before the play.) // I stop in the left turn lane at an intersection // Red light // Large truck in the left turn lane opposite me: I can't see any oncoming traffic // Green light // Truck turns to its left; I begin my own left turn (when I see the truck move, I read the light as if it were a green arrow) // Suddenly, I see two cars barreling down on me // Since I can't get out of the way of either one, I stop in the middle of the two oncoming lanes // The approaching cars screech to a stop, one avoiding me on its left, one on its right // NO CONTACT // The car immediately in front of me moves to my left // I proceed on my way, thinking myself lucky.

"STATE OFFICER": I go 2 blocks, and a car pulls in front of me, cuts me off, and stops // Ordinary vehicle; a man gets out and walks to my car // I think maybe he's one of the drivers from the intersection coming to chew me out—"punch me out" also passes through my mind // He has a blue-and-gold patch on the shoulder of his shirt, takes my license and registration, then goes and sits in his car, appearing to write // He comes back to me and starts in with words like "Felony" and "Leaving the scene of an accident" // He says he works "for the State," so he can't give me a ticket; but he'll "notify the Town Police": they'll handle it // He goes his way, I go mine — with a car full of assorted reactions.

REACTIONS in car: **3 Kids: Youngest child,** confused: "That was scary, Grandma." // **Middle one,** concerned: "Are you all right, Poppy?" // **Oldest,** blasé: "I know that guy. He always does stuff like that." // **Robert:** I'm lying low, trying to regain control, doing my usual head trip on all the possible outcomes. I go from the A of "The guy was just putting the fear of God in me" to the Z of such things as "Arrest, Jail, Lawyer, Trial, Conviction, Fine, Imprisonment." I get myself more or less settled mentally by the time of the play, but emotionally, I'm still trembling at the man's theft of my sense of CONTROL. // **Valerie:** She's upset, lying *very* low. (I dread her silence —

142

I know she's quaking.) But after we take the 3 kids home at 9:00 p.m. she talks about it for the 1st time. She weeps. Next day, she's lying totally low. We talk again. She weeps a lot more: she says she'd rather be dead than live in a world I ke this. By the 3rd day, she's calmer, but still depressed. // **But both of us**, in our different ways (I, thinking: she, feeling), are convinced we've been ROBBED of our PEACE — but what we've been robbed of is our ILLUSION of CONTROL.

NOW: Back and forth between the two lessons, to see what they say about that experience:

GNT 1 Peter 2:19 τοῦτο γὰρ χάρις εἰ διὰ συνείδησιν θεοῦ ὑποφέρει τις λύπας πάσχων ἀδίκως (the grief suffered under Jesus' LH control). 20 ποῖον γὰρ κλέος εἰ ἁμαρτάνοντες καὶ κολαφιζόμενοι ὑπομενεῖτε; (grief pecially Valerie — to a rejectior suffered under the RH control of	This experience was a <u>grace</u> // But grace isn't a <u>convenience</u> // Both of us were robbed of our peace, or at least the <u>illusion</u> of peace // Which led us — es-pecially Valerie — to a <u>rejection</u> of the world we actually live in //	↓↓↓ Jesus himself is the [DOOR] // Whoever enters by <u>another way</u> is a <u>thief</u> and a <u>robber</u> — who steals their <u>illusion</u> of control, as did the "police" in the experience I just told you about.	GNT John 10:1 'Αμὴν ἀμὴν λέγω ὑμῖν, ὁ μὴ <u>εἰσερχόμενος</u> διὰ τῆς <u>θύρας</u> εἰς τὴν αὐλὴν τῶν <u>προβάτων</u> ἀλλὰ <u>ἀναβαίνων</u> <u>ἀλλαχόθεν ἐκεῖνος κλέπτης</u> ἐστὶν καὶ λῃστής·

143

others because they have some-thing on us). ἀλλ᾽ εἰ ἀγαθοποιοῦντες καὶ πάσχοντες ὑπομενεῖτε (patience under Jesus' LH control). τοῦτο χάρις παρὰ θεῷ. (grace = God's favor, his approval of us by Jesus' presence in our loss of the illusion of control).

In this world, we're under authorities, powers // [LEFT-HANDED vs. RIGHT-HANDED CONTROL] // They have RH power over us, but we have no RH power over them // So our quest for peace is always being frus-trated // But Jesus saves us in just that kind of world, not from it // By his LH power, Jesus comes to us in our loss of RH control and makes that very loss the place in which he gives us peace // But not "peace of mind" // That's just a gimmick // It always breaks.

Jesus is the Shepherd and Guardian of our lives // He lays down his control for our sakes // And he invites us to join him in that loss by trusting his presence in our own losses // θυρωρός = the Father and the Spirit // Image of Trinity as Doorkeeper // The Son is the Door // the Father sends us the Door // and the Spirit hovers over the Door as we enter Jesus // On the cross, Jesus goes before us into loss of control.

2 ὁ δὲ εἰσερχόμενος διὰ τῆς θύρας ποιμήν ἐστιν τῶν προβάτων. 3 τούτῳ ὁ θυρωρὸς ἀνοίγει, καὶ τὰ πρόβατα τῆς φωνῆς αὐτοῦ ἀκούει καὶ τὰ ἴδια πρόβατα φωνεῖ κατ᾽ ὄνομα καὶ ἐξάγει αὐτά. 4 ὅταν τὰ ἴδια πάντα ἐκβάλῃ, ἔμπροσθεν αὐτῶν πορεύεται, καὶ τὰ πρόβατα αὐτῷ ἀκολουθεῖ, ὅτι οἴδασιν τὴν φωνὴν αὐτοῦ·

21 εἰς τοῦτο γὰρ ἐκλήθητε, ὅτι καὶ Χριστὸς ἔπαθεν ὑπὲρ ἡμῶν ὑμῖν ὑπολιμπάνων ὑπογραμμὸν ἵνα ἐπακολουθήσητε τοῖς ἴχνεσιν αὐτοῦ, 22 ὃς ἁμαρτίαν οὐκ ἐποίησεν οὐδὲ δόλος ἐν τῷ στόματι αὐτοῦ,

Our calling is to follow him into his LH power in our troubles as in his sufferings // We follow the example of our Shepherd and our friend // He doesn't threaten like the police // Jesus on the cross doesn't use any RH power (fight, threaten) to get his control back // He accepts his forsakenness [PS. 22] // a "sheep before his shearers" // But we fear his LH control // We fear it almost more than the police, because it isn't the RH control we want // LH power doesn't solve our problems the way we expect // It gives the peace that passes our understanding, not the peace we know and love, which is the restoration of control over our lives.

The police // Even though, for ourselves, we love to exercise the kind of control they have, we live in fear of it and flee from it // The "voice of others" that we fear, therefore, is actually the voice of God telling us not to fear but to trust him in the Passion of his Son // It's a call to faith.

Jesus gives them a comparison ("parable," παροιμίαν), and as usual, they don't get it // He repeats his assertion that he's the Door // But then, he speaks to them "without a parable" // He says plainly that "all who came before me are thieves and robbers" // 2 Easter: Thomas was trying to know the Mystery of LH power // But when he says

5 ἀλλοτρίῳ δὲ οὐ μὴ ἀκολουθήσουσιν, ἀλλὰ φεύξονται ἀπ' αὐτοῦ, ὅτι οὐκ οἴδασιν τῶν ἀλλοτρίων τὴν φωνήν.

6 Ταύτην τὴν παροιμίαν εἶπεν αὐτοῖς ὁ Ἰησοῦς, ἐκεῖνοι δὲ οὐκ ἔγνωσαν τίνα ἦν ἃ ἐλάλει αὐτοῖς.

7 Εἶπεν οὖν πάλιν ὁ Ἰησοῦς, Ἀμὴν ἀμὴν λέγω ὑμῖν ὅτι ἐγώ εἰμι ἡ θύρα τῶν προβάτων 8 πάντες ὅσοι ἦλθον [πρὸ ἐμοῦ] κλέπται εἰσὶν καὶ λῃσταί, ἀλλ' οὐκ ἤκουσαν αὐτῶν τὰ πρόβατα.

23 ὃς λοιδορούμενος οὐκ ἀντελοιδόρει, πάσχων οὐκ ἠπείλει, παρεδίδου δὲ τῷ κρίνοντι δικαίως·

24 ὃς τὰς ἁμαρτίας ἡμῶν αὐτὸς ἀνήνεγκεν ἐν τῷ σώματι αὐτοῦ ἐπὶ τὸ ξύλον, ἵνα ταῖς ἁμαρτίαις ἀπογενόμενοι τῇ δικαιοσύνῃ ζήσωμεν, οὗ τῷ μώλωπι ἰάθητε

25 ἦτε γὰρ ὡς πρόβατα πλανώμενοι, ἀλλὰ ἐπεστράφητε νῦν ἐπὶ τὸν ποιμένα καὶ ἐπίσκοπον τῶν ψυχῶν ὑμῶν

9 ἐγώ εἰμι ἡ θύρα· δι' ἐμοῦ ἐάν τις εἰσέλθῃ σωθήσεται καὶ εἰσελεύσεται καὶ ἐξελεύσεται καὶ νομὴν εὑρήσει. 10 ὁ κλέπτης οὐκ ἔρχεται εἰ μὴ ἵνα κλέψῃ καὶ θύσῃ καὶ ἀπολέσῃ· ἐγὼ ἦλθον ἵνα ζωὴν ἔχωσιν καὶ περισσὸν ἔχωσιν

Jesus doesn't revile or rail, as we do, at the RH control of the police of his time // Instead, he gives himself over to it in faith // He trusts the voice of God in the voice of circumstances // [CAIAPHAS] // Even the Final Judgment (Matthew 25) is by the LH power of his presence in dire circumstances // We're free, now and forever, only in our loss of control // We're free by his wounds in our wounds // That's what gives us the peace that passes our understanding, not the peace we know and love, which is the restoration of control over our lives.

"My Lord & my God," he gives up RH power and settles in faith for the paradox of peace by giving up control.

But if we trust Jesus to be our Door, and our Shepherd, and our Guardian at all the times of our consternation, and in all the places of our confusion, we have peace // Because we have returned ourselves to him who never left us // Jesus brings us out of our nothings now as he brought us ex nihilo to begin with // And by the LH power of his death and resurrection, he will bring us out of it forever, to life and life abundant.

146

THEREFORE: Whether we're thinking or feeling types, there will always be some point at which each of us will have to deal with being robbed of control—some point at which we can't regain control on our own. [Valerie / Robert]   And yet all of us will finally come to it in death. But Jesus, the Door, the Shepherd and Guardian of our lives, is always there before us, giving us life and life abundant—giving us PEACE!!! All we need to do is trust him in the paradox of faith in his LH power!!!   *In Nomine Patris, etc.*

147

If it was fun for you to compare the differences between those two versions, I'm glad. As I said, I tried to make the second set of notes land somewhere in between bare promptings and a full manuscript — chiefly for your benefit: they wouldn't be all that easy for me to preach from. But if you didn't have the patience to comb through them, I understand. I promise that you won't have to look at another such mare's nest for the rest of this book. At long last, therefore: Enough, Enough, Enough! It's time for each of us to head for our own kind of meal and evening. What I have left for you is an after-dinner treat.

Cigars at Our House

Robert: What'll it be? Dinner dishes first, or cigars?

Valerie: Cigars. I have something I've been waiting to say ever since I read your first draft of the Epilogue while you were fixing dinner. At least I hope it was a first draft. And I hope it's the last draft of *that* I ever see. When you said you were going to write a letter from your Uncle Dudley to the reader, it sounded like fun. But when you made him talk in run-on sentences and leave typos all over the place, you drove me crazy. It was idiotic! And *cold!* And besides, you were just going in circles, repeating things you'd already said. You have to focus your last chapter on one, preferably new and warm, word to the reader. Say it, and *end!*

Robert: Such restraint! I'm glad I got through the meal with my digestion intact. What kind of cigar do you want?

Valerie: An Arturo Fuente. A Churchill. This may take a while.

Robert: I'll join you. Which humidor are they in?

Valerie: The one with the glass top.

Robert: Hold on, I'll be right back. . . . Behold! I'm a nice person again. I even cut yours for you and lit it. Shoot!

Valerie: Look. I'm not being hostile. Just don't interrupt! I feel very strongly about this. In Chapter Ten, you did a nice job with short, friendly jabs at the things preachers do wrong. In the last chapter, you sounded like your relaxed self. But you're ending on the wrong note if you just repeat yourself in illiterate English with no conclusion in sight. I don't know what you think about all that, but . . .

Robert: I do.

Valerie: I said don't interrupt!

Robert: I have to. Seriously. While I was getting the cigars, I decided to go along with you. You're right. So how about this? How about I do an after-dinner conversation between you and me about writing an epilogue? It could be fun; and you could beat up on me till it was warm and glowing. Besides, that way I'll do my own lines and you can speak yours any way you like.

Valerie: You're really serious?

Robert: Absolutely. I think it'll work. Want another glass of wine?

Valerie: Sure. But don't get into the habit of thinking you can interrupt Mother Nature.

Robert: Perish the thought! I'll be right back. . . . Here you are! The fruit of the vine for the flower of my life. Any ideas?

Valerie: Flowery won't cut it. I want the book to end *high,* not in a heap of clichés. Why don't you go back to your subtitle and do the wisdom of the world versus the foolishness of preaching? And don't forget: the closer you get to the end, the toastier you should be.

Robert: Okay. I'll begin by saying what I think about my readers and me. I think I've got them on my side (mostly), so I'm not going to lecture them or throw don'ts at them anymore. What I'll say is . . .

Valerie: Hold it! Get rid of the *them* and talk to *me.* So far, I'm the only reader you've had, so it ought to be easy. I'm a *preacher* right now, got it? Call me *you.* And don't repeat yourself.

Robert: Good enough.

You, my preacher-friend, have been as patient as Job with me in this book — which is not saying a lot, considering all the things Job bellyached about to God. But since we're both in this preaching boat together, I've got a couple of things from my own experience I want to tell you about.

150

I've been around a long time now, thank God. I'm old enough to be your father, if you're under fifty. What I have to say boils down to just one thing: I hope I've helped you *fall in love* with your calling again. I've been lucky. By grace — and by the gift of having worked for several people whose favorite indoor sport was giving me a hard time — I was sometimes limited to two choices in my ministry: I could either love my calling or bitch about it. Since bitching was a bore, I tried loving.

Valerie: Okay. But that was your last complaint, even if it was a mini-bitch.

Robert: To hear is to obey, Madam. I press on.

You may not have had such good (?) luck. Still, since *all* luck is holy (according to Charles Williams), maybe I'm in a position to give you a bit of it. It may come as a surprise to you, but I was raised in the old school of Anglo-Catholic piety: twelve-cylinder devotional engine, manual shift, and no ABS. You had to get your spiritual life rolling on your own — and you skidded a lot, but could never stop. If you ever saw my meditation notebooks from when I was seventeen, you'd find them loaded with *The Practice of Religion* and Jeremy Taylor. I may not have been as chaste as a dewy blossom, but I was self-improving and self-lacerating to a fare-thee-well. I went to Confession with alarming frequency, bearing with me sin-sheets of mind-numbing specificity. I fasted. I prayed (for a time there, I even made Ignatian meditations) — and I spent a great deal of time protesting to Jesus how much I loved him.

Then one day about twenty years ago, when I was saying Mass, I heard myself repeating mentally (in the silence after the Fraction) the "Jesus prayer" I use (which, as you know, ends with "I love you, I love you, I love you"). And all of a sudden, I said to myself, "Hey! That's beside the point! He loves *me!*" So I said, "You love me! You love me! You love me!" — and I've been saying it at the Fraction ever since.

Valerie: Better. Keep up the personal beat.

Robert: I recommend that to you. Too many preachers are trying to *make themselves* lovers, when the thrill of any romance is the blinding realization that *someone else* loves you. Not for your great accomplishments. Not for the terrific person you think you are. Just for nothing! You're loved simply because your lover is crazy about you.

Try to remember that. God in Christ is stark-staring bonkers over you. The Divine Word (or the Divine Wisdom — pick whichever gender suits your preference) doesn't give a fig for all the wonderful things you've done with your existence, or even for the sins you've messed it up with. He or She started loving you into being when you didn't *be* at all. He or She has gone right on loving you into being no matter what lifestyle you screwed yourself into, or out of. And He or She will go on loving you into existence world without end (even if you insist on whining your way into hell) because He or She is stuck on you.

Valerie: Much better.

Robert: So get off the silly, works-righteousness kick of whipping yourself into a frenzy of love, repentance, and good works, and relax into the ministry that's yours by the drawing of this Love and the voice of this Calling. The church didn't make you a preacher, you know. God did. The church only gives licenses (and nowadays, with fashionable abandon, takes them away). It's a lousy outfit to try to get your identity from.

Valerie: Careful!

Robert: Your identity is your Lover, not the persona you've cooked up for yourself. "For me, to live is Christ, and to die is gain." Being bowled over by His or Her love is what's supposed to make you tick in the pulpit. But above all, it's what will make you run to your study when you prepare your sermons. I didn't always do that. I was a pretty laggard lover most of the time — though by my Lover's great tolerance for short-shrift preparation, I did get in some Sundays' worth of fair whacks at the Word. But I was never as wild about my labors of love as I am now at the age of seventy-two. I finally have time (and when I don't, I find it) to *make out* with the Scriptures. My reading has come to consist of little more than a glimpse at the day's *New York Times,* a riffle through the week's *New Yorker,* and The Holy Bible, every day — at increasingly respectable length.

Valerie: Keep warming!

Robert: Love pays terrific wages. My "mental concordance" to the New Testament now is not to the KJV or any other version; it's to the original Greek of the UBS text. (Don't plead ineptitude with me: if I nearly flunked Greek in college and ended up where I am, you can learn to read it if you try.) I've even gone back recently and started to wake up my Rip van Winkle Hebrew after a forty-year sleep. Best of all, I now love exegesis and exposition with a passion I never thought possible.

Valerie learned Greek about ten years ago. Ever since, she's followed (in the original) the daily readings at Mass while I translate. Lately, though, with fantastic patience, she reads me the Old Testament lessons in English (three or four words at a time) as I slog through the *Biblia Hebraica Stuttgartensis*, not with gun and camera but with groping grammar, shaky syntax, and a magnifying glass to help me make out the Masoretic pointing. Sometimes it takes us (me!) twenty minutes to get through ten verses. Still, she's a peach. When she has a migraine, she does get antsy at my dithering. But she hangs in there.

Valerie: Thank you, Sir.

Robert: But best of all are the times when we're at the end of a reading and one of us spots something neither has noticed before. Or when one of us asks, "What on earth does that mean?" — and off we go into the sheer fun of *playing* with the Scriptures.

Valerie: You're right. That really is the best.

Robert: I know what you're thinking. That kind of exegetical duet sounds worlds away from anything you've ever done, *chez* any *nous* you've ever managed to install yourself in. You want to say to me, "Whoa, there! I can't just transfer your life into mine. What do you want from me?" Calm down! I'm not talking about transfer here. I'm talking about the hardest fact of love: somehow, somewhere, somewhen, you have to give it *time.*

Valerie: That's yummy! You're almost there!

Robert: I don't want anything *from* you. I want the best *for* you. I want you to be wild about your calling. If you were head over heels in love with some guy or gal who just waltzed in on you, you'd carry on nonstop about it — and bore everybody else silly with your infatuation. *Infatuation*, though, is from the root *FA*, "speak": *in*-fatuated, therefore, means *speechless* with love. That's the great paradox. That's the foolishness of preaching which the wisdom of the world will never understand: As Saul couldn't see his calling until he was struck blind, so you will never hear yours again until you've been struck dumb by the love of him with whom you have to do.

Only in dumb *love* will you ever be able to speak. Only in the deadness of your mind to everything that isn't Jesus, silent in his death, will you ever be able to hear and proclaim the authentic Word. "The hour is coming and now is, when the *dead* will hear the voice of the Son of God, and they that hear shall live." Only in the deafness of your death will you hear that *Ephphatha!* which opens your ears to the Gospel.

But since I've said all that before, I just wish you well. I've always liked clergy. They're lucky. To the degree that they love the Lover who calls them, they can be the freest people on earth. So *Shalom!* to you in your freedom. Χάρις ὑμῖν καὶ εἰρήνη πληθυνθείη (1 Peter 1:2). Relax into the lovely liberty with which Christ has made you free.

Have a cigar!